Travelling with Soldiers and Bishops

Mathew Haumann M.H.M.

Travelling with Soldiers and Bishops

Stories of Struggling People in Sudan

Paulines Publications Africa

PAULINES PUBLICATIONS AFRICA
Daughters of St Paul
P.O. Box 49026
00100 Nairobi GPO (Kenya)

Typesetting and Layout by Mukundi Miringu

Cover Design by Lawrence Mbugua

Printed by Kolbe Press, P.O. Box 468, 00217 Limuru (Kenya)

Paulines Publications Africa is an activity of the Daughters of St Paul, an international religious congregation, using the press, radio, TV and films to spread the gospel message and to promote the dignity of all people.

Contents

Dedication

I dedicate this book to the many people
who were willing to share their stories with me,
without them this book
would have never been written.

SUDAN

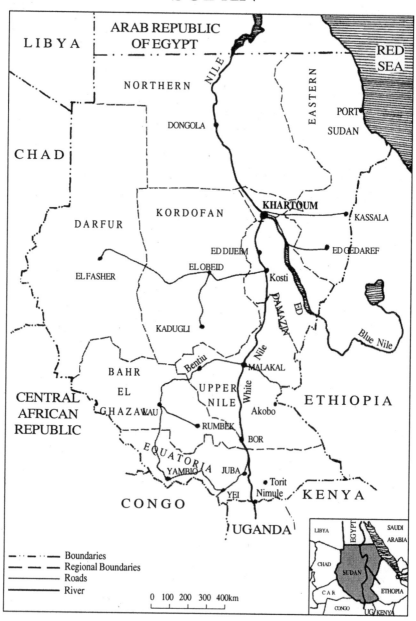

List of Abbreviations

CSI	Christian Solidarity Internationalis
DOT	Diocese of Torit
FACE Foundation	Friends of African Children's Education Foundation
GOS	Government of Sudan
GUSCO	Gulu Support the Children Organisation
IDP	Internally Displaced People
JRS	Jesuit Refugee Service
LRA	Lord's Resistance Army
NSCC	New Sudan Council of Churches
PLE	Primary Leaving Examination
SPLA/M	Sudan Peoples Liberation Army/Movement
SRRA	Sudan Relief and Rehabilitation Association
UNEB	Uganda National Examination Board
UNICEF	United Nations Children's Fund
UPDF	Ugandan Peoples Defence Force
USAP	Union of Sudanese African Parties
CEAWA	Commission for the Eradication of Women and Children's Abduction
SCC	Sudan Council of Churches
OLS	Operation Lifeline Sudan

Foreword

People are too often inclined to think the situation in Sudan hopeless. To think like that is a luxury which only those who can get away from Sudan can afford. As Sudanese we cannot afford to think the situation is hopeless. We haven't given up on our country or on our people. This book is a plea to support the Sudanese in their struggle for education and peace. We Sudanese believe that there are possibilities, despite many of our friends' apparent lack of faith in the Sudan.

That is why I am happy that Fr Mathew Haumann, the author, has published this book in the series "Faith in Sudan." He has not lost faith in Sudan. He has begun to share our faith, after thinking for a long time that he himself had to bring the faith to us. He knows that our faith is strong and that we are willing to share it. Many of the characters of this book we have visited together, in Sudan, Kenya, Uganda and the U.S. Mathew has witnessed their struggle and their faith; we encouraged them, but more often they encouraged us with their strength and faith.

In the Madi language we call a missionary like Mathew *"Munduku ba."* It means that although coming from outside, he is a human being like us, and has become one of us. The stories in the book are his as much as ours.

At times I compare missionaries to bees. They left their hives in Europe or America. I want to underscore an aspect of bee life other than their work. Bees fly from flower to flower. They spread the pollen, fertilise the plants and help them bear fruit. Africa is full of beautiful flowers of faith, and partly due to the work of missionaries our faith has born fruit and has grown strong and sweet.

But bees not only fertilise flowers. They also go back to the hives whence they came, laden with honey. This book contains some of the honey that we offer to the world: our struggle for peace and education against many odds.

The war has crushed us under heavy burdens; it has stolen the youth of our children, and many of us are traumatised. But with peace coming, our situation is not hopeless. We have our faith in God, in our people and also in the people who have not lost faith in Sudan.

Bishop Paride Taban

War Children

*"He who does not know the hardships of
a soldier at war says, 'They went a-soldiering,'
although they went to die for us."*

(Akan proverb)

When, new to Sudan, I visited Khartoum in 1988, a fellow traveller from the North made me understand that the war between the government in the North and the SPLA rebels in the South would end soon with the crushing of the rebels. It did not take me long to discover that not everybody agreed. Many hoped, but few believed, that the SPLA would defeat the government. Twenty years later, peace efforts which often failed before, seem finally to be succeeding. But peace is more than absence of war.

The people and organisations behind the efforts will tell you, with that tired look in their eyes, that the war in Sudan is a complex affair. And the longer I listen to those who pretend to know, the more I realise that it is not one war but many, and that new ones are being started every now and then. Different times and different people tell their own version of the truth.

A few months after my arrival I met the first SPLA freedom fighter. He told me that, just as they had fought in the colonial days to get independence from Britain, they were now fighting the Arabs from the North who were trying to re-colonise the South. He blamed Britain for the war, for handing over the South to the northern Arabs at the time of independence in 1956. I believe that non-Sudanese play a role in this war, but to put all the blame on them is a bit too easy, and most Sudanese know it.

A few years later I lived in the SPLA held area. One of the commanders told me that I, as a Christian, had to be on the side of the SPLA, because this war was a war between the northern Muslims and the southern Christians plus traditionalists. I have never felt comfortable with that analysis of the war; religious wars never stop. When I pointed out that African Muslims were also being killed by government soldiers, he did not deny it. The analysis of the war shifted from religious to ethnic. Culture and religion do play a significant role, as they are thoroughly used and abused. The Arabs try to impose their culture on the whole country through a concerted effort to islamise the entire population.

The war has often been explained to me as a racial conflict between Arabs and Africans. A determined soldier said, "This war will only end when we are acknowledged as human beings, and no longer seen as slaves." It was obvious that he was prepared for a long war.

For many years the war was forgotten. The Western world hardly paid much attention to it. But with the beginning of the extraction of the recently discovered oil in many areas of the South, it became obvious to many, inside and outside Sudan, that the war was also about oil, a resource worth fighting for.

There are smaller wars within the big one. In the South, different factions of the SPLA have been fighting each other. But also in the North the government faces armed opposition from people in Darfur and the Bedja.

By the time I had also been convinced of this complexity, I was stopped one day at one of the many roadblocks on a so-called road in Southern Sudan. A young boy stuck a Kalashnikov through the window and demanded copybooks and ballpoints for himself and his fellow soldiers. A few of his friends were sitting by the roadside. The pieces of army uniform they were wearing were too big for them, as were their weapons. When a gun is pointed at me, I am usually very cooperative; I give what is demanded, if I have it. And I did have some copybooks and pens in the car, which turned me into a bit of a good guy in the eyes of the young soldier and his friends. They were all standing around the car checking for other valuables. There were other things, but they seemed happy with the copybooks and pens. The rest I was allowed to keep. As we were by now on speaking terms I did not feel threatened any longer. We got to talking. The young man withdrew the rifle and started explaining that this war was about education. The government wanted to keep the southerners uneducated. It is easier to suppress and enslave the uneducated. The government had ruined the educational system in the South, that is why he and other child-soldiers were fighting for education in Sudan. Neither he nor his friends wanted to flee again to Ethiopia or to Kenya to get education. It was clear that he truly believed what he said. His war was a war for education, therefore not complex but very simple. If he won, he would go to school, get education and manage his life in this beautiful country. He was still a child, but his truth was no less true than the explanations I had heard from adults. Ever so often I hear new ones.

For us adults, the complexity is made up of land, water, oil, human rights and religion, issues affecting the whole country. The weapons used are very diverse. Tanks, bomber aircraft, helicopter gunships, mines, firearms and ammunition are mainly supplied by the Western world, which makes us accomplices in the war. Less conventional weapons used in the war are hunger, displacement of people, and abduction of women and children. Constant displacements uproot people from their homes and culture. They lose their identity.

Not providing basic education or ruining the educational system in the South is felt as a greater damage to society than bombings, however big the panic they create among the people. While the government knows that it is easier to suppress the uneducated, the SPLA does not have a great record either in providing education for the youth. In the early years of the war education was not a priority, as there was no time to institutionalise even a *de facto* government. But often it is easy to conscript the uneducated, because the youth have no other choice. This war has produced unconventional fighters, young children. Other children are captured and abducted as slaves.

The present civil war started in 1983. After such a long time the world seems to have become discouraged and lost interest. A whole generation has grown up without experiencing peace. Only some aspects still attract attention, like an umpteenth round of peace talks. On one occasion the fact that slavery still exists may be highlighted; on another the news that the SPLA has handed over 2,500 child-soldiers to Unicef hits the headlines. It is often forgotten that most victims in this war are women and children dragged into the war or getting entangled without being able to get out. And yet these very children are the future of Sudan.

The stories in this book are about some of the victims of this long war. Many have lost their lives. Nearly all have lost their youth. People who know of my regular trips to South Sudan often ask me whether I know any child soldiers. The war in Sudan affects the whole society, children included. I hardly know any children in Sudan who don't play war or war games. They play at being soldiers, but unfortunately it does not remain a game for very long. They have to take part in actual fighting, usually becoming victims themselves by being forced to victimise others.

Child-soldiers have been used in Sudan, by the government as well as by the SPLA, since 1983. Sudan is certainly not the only country in Africa, or in the world, where child-soldiers fight wars. With a whole society involved in war, children are not exempt.

That was the case also in our own society, before our wars became long distance and computerised affairs. When our soldiers were still marching on foot we called them the "infantry," from the word "infant", a child. Children are naturally inclined to imitate adult behaviour, and if they don't want to join, they are often lured or forced into taking part in war.

It is estimated that more than 300,000 children are taking part in armed conflicts in different countries. Often these estimates are on the low side, for there are no clear definitions of "child-soldier" and the clear definitions drafted at a UN conference are not always understood in the rural areas of Sudan.

Army leaders know that in some ways children are near-ideal soldiers. They are small, quick and fearless. Unlike adult soldiers, many don't fear death. They can easily be manipulated and are often proud to receive difficult assignments which adults would be hesitant to carry out. I heard it said; "After training they are the best fighting machine a commander can wish for himself."

I have at times watched the army of the SPLA going to the front, travelling on foot where no vehicles could go, even if they had them. The soldiers lead the long procession travelling through the night, so as not to be seen from the air and to avoid the heat of the day. The war nearly looked like a family affair, with everybody being given the proper role. The men led; women, children and cattle followed. The children carried food, drove the cattle or perhaps shouldered ammunition for their fathers. Were they child-soldiers? They were on their way to the front much as they would be on the way to cattle camps in peace time.

One young boy was not yet involved in the war. He carried only a small lamb, as he would when at home. Some people might be inclined to call herding cattle by young boys child labour. Children do what their parents do. Where the adults fight a war, so do children. Not that I underestimate the harmful effects on children involved in war. The stories in this book should make that clear. I only want to point out that we cannot separate the problem of child-soldiers from the war itself.

The only way to stop the use and abuse of children in the war is to stop the war.

In Africa children seem to be part of every war and usually they are the main victims. As the result of war children have been displaced or separated from their families by searching for education. They become soldiers for a variety of reasons; some boys grow up next to their soldier fathers, as mentioned above. Others are forcibly recruited, one could say kidnapped. Girls are often sexually abused. But others follow the soldiers because they get something to eat. At times they are even used by the armies to attract food and other aid. As many aid organisations, even Unicef, know, disadvantaged children are good fundraisers. We have given them many names; unaccompanied minors, slaves, lost boys, orphans, displaced, sex slaves, refugees. These terms are often invented for fundraising campaigns. A young boy put it like this: "They call me 'refugee,' but I never fled. I have been blown away like the leaf of a tree. A strong wind arose, full of fire and terror, and one day I was blown away from home." Through the terrible wind of the war many children have been blown away from home all over Sudan and the wider world.

Of course the world condemns children victimisation. Article 1 of the Universal Declaration of Human Rights states that, "All human beings are born free and equal in dignity and rights." Children make up a special component of the human family. They certainly need our support to have their fundamental right to life, liberty and security of person acknowledged (Article 3), the right to be free of any form of slavery or servitude (Article 4), the right not to be subjected to torture or to cruel, inhuman or degrading treatment or punishment (Article 5), the right to a nationality (Article15). Many Sudanese children clamour for these rights. Especially in the Southern Sudan children and their parents wish they got the right to education (Article 26). It is good to read what the Sudanese think about education in peace time. Education shall be free and compulsory, at least at the primary level. Education will promote general culture, to enable the child, on the basis of equal opportunity, to develop abilities, individual judgement, and a sense of moral and social responsibility, so as to become a useful member of society. It all remains very much of a dream.

What has contributed most to the use of child-soldiers in Sudan has certainly been the collapse of educational opportunities. Many of them were even lured into becoming child-soldiers with promises of education for which they were prepared to travel great distances, leaving their homes and at times their country. I met them in Sudan, Ethiopia, Kenya, Uganda, Europe and the USA.

Child or ex-child-soldiers are not the only children victims of the war. In raids on villages women and children have often been abducted and sold as slaves. Many children have been refugees their whole lives, living in refugee camps, without ever living in a place they could call home. Others lucky enough to stay in Sudan have been traumatised by the constant bombing raids and displacements.

In the stories that follow I shall introduce the reader to some of the children I have met and who have told me part of their story. The stories have touched me and I know that the children have not shared them with me for my own sake. In Africa stories are told to be passed on. They do not tell the life of only one individual. Such a life is often that of thousands of people, of a community trying to survive the war in Sudan. My concern is not only with the truth of the stories. Some facts might even have been distorted by the people who told me their story, or indeed by myself as I am aware of not having a very exact mind. But I have tried to listen to what these children truly experienced. Facts alone are not the whole truth. The context often explains what it truly means to be a child or a young soldier in this war. I have often changed the names, at times to protect the individual but also because they are not stories of individual boys or girls. They are stories of thousands of children, many of whom cannot tell them anymore. The stories of the dead are remembered in Africa even when the dead are not called by name.

Many ask how to stop the use of child-soldiers in this war, how to see to it that the children get what is their right. How can we supply at least basic education for children? The answer is simple but not easy to accomplish: stop the war. If there is peace, the abduction and use of child-soldiers will disappear, or at least can be addressed, and a basic education system can once again take off in Southern Sudan. Without peace the children will be the first to lose their youth prematurely and they will be powerless to defend their human rights. Human rights violations will not come to an end until the war does. We cannot separate the two. If we care about the plight of children, we must do everything possible to end the war and these horrible practices. As Archbishop Desmond Tutu said, "It is immoral that adults should use children to fight their wars for them. There is simply no excuse, no acceptable argument for arming children."

Blessed Damian School

*"The person who is not the parent of the child
is the one who is fit to bring it up."*

(Ugandan proverb)

This morning Abdul came to collect me in Kampala. He was happy to drive me to Kyatiri. For him it was an opportunity to visit his family. Kyatiri is not far from Masindi, about 230 km from Kampala. Abdul drives fast, assuring me that it won't take more than three hours to get there. Coming from Sudan, Uganda looks really prosperous to me. Along the road there are lots of shops and markets, and loads of advertisements for anything one can think of. Coca Cola, beer and cigarettes are certainly top of the list. But the many ads for soap give me the impression that an effort is being made to keep Uganda clean. The further away from Kampala the fewer ads I see, although Coca Cola and the painkiller Hedex reach pretty far. But even where there are no more ads the country looks promising, green, lush and fertile. Everywhere the fields abound with bananas, sweet potatoes, coffee and cassava. Not far from Kyatiri we leave the tarmac and soon we see a sign "Blessed Damian School, three kilometres." It has rained and the road is rather slippery, but Abdul is a good driver.

Then, among the trees, we see the school, or rather a school complex. Abdul points out to me first the secondary school, the boys' dormitories, the school garden, girls' dormitories, the sports fields and staff housing. We enter the compound of the primary school, with more classrooms, dormitories and a kitchen.

As we stop by a prefabricated building serving as convent, Sr Sophie welcomes us. It is a warm welcome and we take our time over it. "Good greetings are better than a good bed", an African proverb says. Sr Sophie and I haven't seen each other for a long time, but we have common memories of Sudan. In 1992, when we last met, she was the head teacher of a primary boarding school for girls in the Imotong Mountains of Southern Sudan.

Sr Sophie and her congregation of the Missionary Sisters of Mary Mother of the Church helped restart education in the liberated area of Eastern Equatoria. The education system had practically collapsed during the war and the government did not seem very interested in providing education. Others would put it a lot stronger, alleging that the government deliberately wants to keep the people uneducated, as it is easier to exploit and suppress the uneducated. Even in colonial days education in the South was left very much to the Churches. The Churches wanted to get involved in education, and for the colonial government it was a cheap way of providing some education for the people in Southern Sudan. After independence the government wanted to impose Arabic culture in the South through education in Arabic. It proceeded to expel the missionaries from the South, among other reasons for the role they played in education, which was conducted in English. But even after their expulsion, many missionaries joined the refugees from the south in Uganda, the Congo and Central African Republic. They opened schools there, or sponsored the Southern Sudanese students for primary and secondary education.

The sisters started working in the diocese of Torit in 1985, but when the war around there escalated in 1988 they had to go back to Uganda to wait for better times. The bishop and the sisters considered these better times had come when the SPLA liberated the town. By 1990, the town was liberated by the SPLA. Moreover the bishop

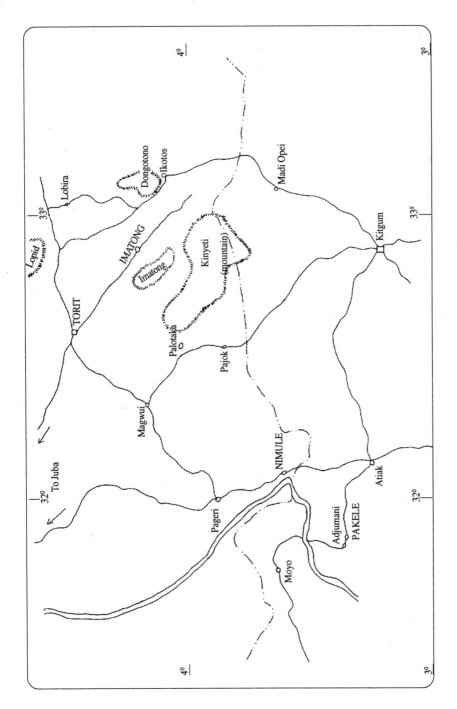

and three of his priests had been released from prison, where they had been held for a hundred days in what the SPLA called "protective custody." Even if the Church and the SPLA did not always agree on the methods of serving the people, they realised that they needed each other.

With the bishop and his council, the sisters looked for areas where their help was most needed and wanted. The SPLA and the Churches both saw the importance of education. The SPLA tried to start a few schools, but they did not receive much support from the outside world. Moreover many of the teachers had been drafted into the SPLA army. The movement welcomed any assistance the Church could give. The SPLA did not consider education for girls a priority. The diocese of Torit was hesitant to start a boarding school for boys, as they were afraid that the SPLA might come and press-gang them into service when they needed more soldiers at the front.

Bishop Paride Taban and his council did see the importance of education for girls and women and with the sisters they started an intertribal boarding school for girls in Torit. Educating children of different tribes together was seen as a means of building peace between these tribes. Their effort aimed at assisting the people of the diocese of Torit to rebuild their lives in the liberated area of Sudan. People were happy. There was hope again. Sr Sophie was teaching in Torit when I arrived there for the first time in 1990.

However, the Khartoum government was not at all happy about losing Torit to the SPLA. A Russian-built Antonov bomber flew over regularly and occasionally bombed the town. It was terrifying, and we dug shelters next to our houses. Trenches were dug next to the hospital and the school. We had been told that we were relatively safe as long as we were lying below ground level during the bombings. The children were the first to hear the plane, and some dogs seemed to hear them even before the children. They could distinguish the sound of the Antonov from the sound of a cargo plane on its way to Juba. We had regular bomb-alerts. The

SPLA received a radio message when a bomber was in the air, but they did not know where it would go to. The alarm was rung and everybody was on the alert. We would sigh with relief when learning a few hours later that the bomber had gone to drop its bombs elsewhere. We were safe for another day. Living in Torit was nerve-wracking but bearable.

On June 5th, 1991, everything changed. Sr Sophie will never forget that day. The children heard the Antonov and started running to the shelters. The bombs exploded all around. When the explosions stopped and the sisters and the children got up, twenty-one people around them were dead and many more wounded. Sr Sophie and the children had reached their shelter just in time; the sisters, as usual, had warned the children in good time. Torit mourned its dead, but the people were scared and the next day many of them started leaving the town for safer places in the hills. Nor did the sisters feel too safe, and they felt responsible for the safety of the girls in their care. They wondered whether the time had come for them to leave the town, like so many other people did.

They talked with the bishop and looked for places where they could go. From Torit they could see the Imotong mountains in the far distance and they heard from the parish priest that there was a small church plot at the foot of the mountains. They moved to Imotong, forty kilometres from Torit. At the foot of the beautiful mountains they built a new home. The mountains provided some security against bombing raids. There was a tiny school but no teachers. It looked like a suitable spot where the sisters could settle, at least temporarily. After all, missionaries are not supposed to settle down. There was no convent, and this was no time to build one. Nobody knew what turn the war would take even in a few months. And the idea of the tented convent was born, with four tents for the sisters and one for a visitor. Two larger tents served as the community and dining room and as chapel respectively. The new compound was erected in a few days. It was all very rudimentary but would do for the time being. Most of the pupils had followed the sisters from Torit to Imotong. The sisters started their own school garden with the help of the Bishop and the local people. The Bishop asked me to consider Imotong as my weekend parish, where I would go on Friday evening to return on Sunday evening or Monday morning. In that way the sisters would be able to attend the Eucharist at least a few times a week and on Sunday I would celebrate the eucharist in the small church that the people had built. I felt a lot safer in Imotong than in Torit, where we still had regular bomb alerts and an actual bombing every six or seven weeks. I always looked forward to a weekend in Imotong. The Imotong School soon became a centre for education for girls from Eastern Equatoria.

But good times seldom last long in Southern Sudan. In 1992 the government recaptured Torit. I was safely in Holland but the sisters had to run and flee with the girls towards the Uganda border. For a short time Sr Sophie and Sr Rita tried to restart their school in Nimule but the pupils did not feel safe. The war front was still close. The school was not a girls' school anymore; it also catered for boys. The sisters found it very trying when the SPLA forcibly recruited some older boys. Sr Sophie felt that the time had come to protect the children from the war. One sister went with some of the children to Narus where the sisters are running the St Bakhita primary and secondary school to this day. The churches are struggling to keep education going in Southern Sudan but often they receive little support. The donor agencies do not consider education a priority, but the Sudanese see educated children as the hope for the future. Many southern Sudanese have fled to Uganda. It is true that the north of Uganda is not that much safer than south Sudan. It might even be more dangerous. But the Southern Sudanese have fled not only from the dangers of the war but also to get for their children the education that they cannot get at home. The UNHCR supports education for refugees, but there is hardly any support for education for the displaced within Sudan.

Sr Sophie eventually joined a group of Sudanese refugees in Uganda to look after some of the girls who were with her in Imotong.

She found it hard to leave others behind. It had not been easy to educate the displaced while being constantly displaced yourself. The sisters had tried to act as parents to the children, often not knowing where the real parents were. Sr Sophie needed a break from having to care for children, whom she had to leave again after a short time. She changed profession and for some time worked as financial administrator for the DOT in the refugee camps of Pakele and Adjumani in the north of Uganda. In this capacity she also was in charge of the sponsorship programme of the diocese. She paid school fees for the children who had nobody to pay them, but she felt strongly that they needed more than just school fees. She started looking after some of them and soon enough she asked the bishop to let her get back into education or at least to work with children who needed tutelage. They were not really orphans but in the refugee camps they were alone, and Sr Sophie cared for them, at times as a gentle mother but at other times as a challenging father.

Now Sr Sophie is the headmistress of Blessed Damian School. She and bishop Paride have named this school Blessed Damian after the Belgian priest Damian de Veuster who worked among the lepers of Molokai. The lepers at that time were the outcasts of society. People were afraid of them. In some ways the ex-child-soldiers here in this school also feel a bit like outcasts. The armies whence they fled look at them as deserters, and their society is afraid of them because people see them as murderers. Only their immediate family will see them forever as their beloved sons who were forcibly taken to war. Not many people see them as victims of the war, as wounded young people who are badly traumatised and who need healing.

Sr Sophie is more than a headmistress. She is a founder of this school together with Bishop Paride Taban. As we sit in the shade of a big tree she tells me about her adventure from the time we were together in the Imotong hills. She shares how some of the children had followed her from Torit, trusting that she could provide education. She talked to the bishop and they came to the conclusion that they needed their own school for Sudanese children. Sr Sophie knew many of these children and Bishop Taban told her about the request of Commander Yousif Kuwa of the Nuba mountains to help him find education for boys who had travelled for months to south Sudan for this purpose. They had hoped to find it in Palotaka, in the school of the Face Foundation. But when they arrived the Face Foundation had nothing to offer except war, hunger and jiggers. The war had ruined the plans for this school and Palotaka was abandoned when the war came too close.

In 1996 Sr Sophie and Bishop Taban started this school in Kyatiri. At first they wanted a school for 56 boys from the Nuba Mountains who got caught up in the war in Sudan while hoping to get education. They needed a safe place, where they would not be picked up again to be sent to the front. They were dubbed "unaccompanied minors." Children should be accompanied, and these boys were lucky that Bishop Taban and Sr Sophie were willing to be with them for some time. The UNHCR, which did not want them to leave the refugee camp, changed its mind when the camp was attacked by the LRA, the Lord's Resistance Army in the north of Uganda. They were even willing to provide a few planes to airlift the boys and a few girls to Masindi, the nearest airstrip to Kyatiri. Bishop Taban went with the first group in a small plane, it was an exciting experience for the boys who never had flown, something like flying to freedom, away from the war. But on landing at Masindi they did not get a warm reception. The authorities there decided that refugees belong in camps, so they were arrested and imprisoned for half a day. The bishop kept his cool, talking and phoning to people sympathetic with the victims of the war in Sudan. He knew that President Museveni of Uganda was one of them. He knew people who knew people who could contact the president, and in the end orders came from Museveni himself that they should be allowed to go to Kyatiri.

Both the bishop and Sr Sophie knew the plight of these boys who needed more than a school. Sr Sophie says: "Our objective with this school was to give these boys a home, to give them guidance, to give them a foundation to build their life on. We were also willing to provide them with a good academic education. After all that was what they had left their homes for. But a lot had happened since then and we knew part of what they had gone through. Many had died. They felt betrayed by the SPLA, they had the feeling that nobody cared for them except this commander Yousif Kuwa. We were aware that these children needed healing above all. But we did not exclude that they could not get healed whilst studying English and mathematics. On asking them what they wanted most they answered education and football, so that is what I started with, education and football. We began with two teachers, teaching mornings and evenings. One of our cooks was the widow of a commander of the Nuba Mountains who had died in the war, but the students themselves are also very willing to cook. They work in the school garden but they also have their own garden and the school buys their produce. In this way they experience that there is a reward for hard work. We made sure that there was time for football." The students trust her, she certainly is not somebody to spoil them but she stays close to them. She knows: "If the master does not take care of the goat pen, the goats will die of disease."

The Sisters of Mary Mother of the Church, the mission congregation to which Sr Sophie belongs, gave them 25 hectares of land. Friends of Sr Emmanuella[1] in Belgium provided the first instalment for a few zinc prefab halls, which would function as classrooms and dormitory and a prefab house which could function as a convent. The food was provided by the World Food Programme. The Sisters felt it important that there should be a mix with young people who had had an ordinary youth, and so they allowed the children from the neighbourhood to become day pupils. In this way they also got the goodwill of the people from the area.

A few hours later Sr Sophie showed me around the schools and introduced me to some of her pupils. She told me that by now they

[1] A group of people in Belgium who started an organisation to support the work of Sister Emmanuella in Egypt. Later on they also started supporting other projects in the Third World.

have pupils from all over Sudan and the north of Uganda. As she is being called away, she introduces me to one of the older boys. James is from Wau in Sudan, and joined the SPLA when he was still very young. Many call him Sergeant James, as he moves like a drilled soldier spotlessly dressed in a well ironed shirt and trousers. On inquiring, he tells me that he actually held the rank of a sergeant on leaving the SPLA after having seen enough action. He certainly believes in the cause for which the SPLA is fighting but he had his own reasons for leaving the army. He agrees to talk, although he believes that only those who have been at the front can understand.

"I was proud to be promoted to sergeant in the SPLA. However this meant leading soldiers to the Yei front quite often. We were a well-trained group and won many battles. Some combatants used to count how many men they had killed. My job was to report how many we had lost. Dead enemies were not important to me, but how can one forget a dead friend? We lost quite a number in battle. But that was not the worst.

During a night battle the government troops encircled us, but we managed to slip away except for one of us who was captured. We knew that the government soldiers often tortured prisoners of war, before killing them, so we followed them to liberate our friend. From behind a rock we saw five of them pass. It was dark, but there was enough light to see them move. I gave the order to fire and we shot the lot. When there was no more motion we went closer, to find four government soldiers and our friend whom we were trying to liberate, all dead. It is hard to remain a soldier when you lose all your friends."

That was when Sergeant James left the SPLA and became a student at Blessed Damian. Later they told me that he is not one of the best students, and that his health is not so good either. But how can he be a good student with so many friends to mourn?

Sr Sophie comes back. She tells me that quite a few of her pupils were in Ethiopia, and she is sure that I could have met some in the past when visiting the returning refugees from Ethiopia in the early 1990s.

This visit with Sr Sophie took place a few years ago. The school has now grown into a primary and secondary school. Sr Sophie has been transferred to another school, but she is not forgotten. Of course with the increase in the number of students, and with new teachers who don't know the Sudanese background of their pupils, personal care has diminished. Moreover one cannot expect every teacher to be a good counsellor for the traumatised; we are not even sure of what that means in these circumstances. The school has no special programmes for de-traumatisation, no special focus on emotional wounds. Workshops are being organised for the teachers and staff on how they can support traumatised pupils. They don't use the term "traumatised" but they talk about "living in difficult circumstances," and nearly all the students from Sudan have known difficult circumstances The sisters and other teachers try to establish a sense of normality, providing a good education together with "normal" children from Uganda. The school is a kind of safe haven where the children from Sudan can feel secure enough to reconsider their past and where education gives them some hope for the future. This hope helps them to cope. They follow the peace talks, they miss their home but we are not sure that they can return or want to return to Sudan as soon as peace is signed.

Sr Sophie knew what these children had gone through. During a visit a few years ago I asked her to tell me more. But she thought that introducing me was enough. It was up to the students to decide what they wanted to tell me. She knew that there was a lot to tell, for she had listened to their stories as part of their healing process. With a smile she added, "Maybe they will tell you a different story from the one they told me, or they will tell the same story in a different way, for a European to understand."

A Child-Soldier

"He who runs from the white ant,
may stumble upon the stinging ant."

(Nigerian proverb)

Last night Michael hesitantly put up his hand when I asked who had been in Pochala in 1991 when I landed there with Bishop Taban. We had gone there to welcome the thousands of what were then called "unaccompanied minors." These mostly young boys had just returned from Ethiopia where they had lived as refugees for several years. But in 1991 they were no longer welcome in Ethiopia after the fall of Mengistu. His regime and the SPLA had been supporting each other. The term "unaccompanied minors" was probably invented by fundraisers; others called them "orphans" in the hope that some organisation or other would take pity on them. But these boys were accompanied by their guardians from the SPLA, by their teachers and by quite a few church personnel.

At that time Bishop Taban was the chairman of the fledgling New Sudan Council of Churches, of which I was the first employee. When we heard about the hundreds of thousands of refugees returning from Ethiopia. I was asked to attend the Nairobi meeting of UN and NGO personnel to see what could be done.

It was a tedious meeting; as they were back in their own country, these refugees were technically no longer refugees, and there-

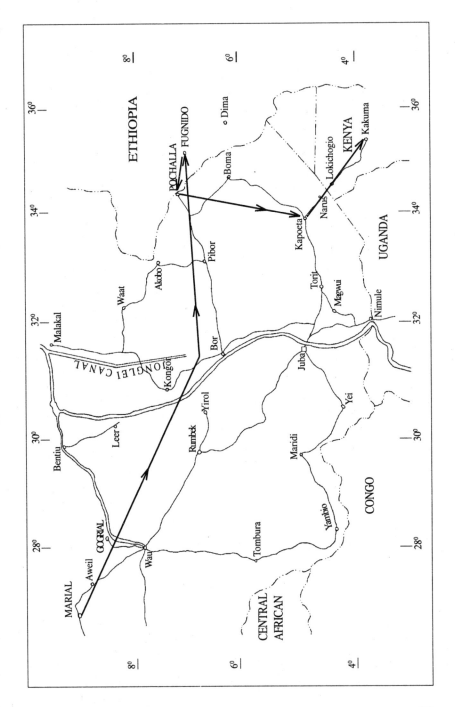

ETHIOPIA

POCHALLA
FUGNIDO
o Dima

o Boma

KENYA
Lokichogio
Kakuma
Narus
Kapoeta

UGANDA

Pibor

Akobo

Waat

Torit
Magwui
Nimule

JONGLEI CANAL

Malakal

Kongor

Bor

Juba

Yirol

Yei

Leer

Rumbek

Bentiu

Maridi

CONGO

COGRIAL

Wau

Tombura

Yambio

MARIAL
Aweil

CENTRAL
AFRICAN

36°
34°
32°
30°
28°

8°
6°
4°

fore no longer the responsibility of the UNHCR. They were "internally displaced" and thus left to the care of NGOS and the churches. Relief work has become an industry. I got the impression that there was a competition afoot about who would get the biggest piece of the cake of misery in Southern Sudan. Various organisations were nearly fighting over who should care for these so-called "unaccompanied minors." Many organisations saw these boys, who were supposed to have gone to Ethiopia to be educated, as prime fundraising material. I knew that we, as NSCC, had no funds, no planes, no personnel to do anything much for these people. I returned home, accepting that we would have to leave them in the care of foreign NGOS, who had the funds, the logistics and the personnel. They were chartering planes to assess the situation, and taking journalists along to get the right publicity for their fundraising.

I returned to Torit a bit discouraged, and told the bishop that we had nothing to offer to these returnees from Ethiopia. But Bishop Taban seemed to think differently. He said, "You are working with the Churches in Sudan. The returnees are our own people, our own brothers and sisters, our own children, and we can never leave them to foreign NGOS or the UN. You should have been there at the Ethiopian border to welcome them." He was of course right, but I protested. We were empty-handed and had very little to offer, but the argument cut no ice with the bishop who pointed out that it is easier to shake hands with people when our hands are empty. I had no answer to that, which did not make it any easier to be empty-handed. Moreover the fact that I was working with the Sudanese Churches did not make a Sudanese of me and I wondered aloud whether I could truly represent the Sudanese Churches. I was glad that in the end Bishop Taban agreed to go with me, first to Nasir and then to Pochala, both on the Ethiopian border, where some hundred thousand Sudanese refugees were crossing the border to return to Sudan.

It was the rainy season and only an Ethiopian pilot dared to land with the Twin Otter plane of the UN on the muddy Pochala airstrip. Other pilots did not dare land there as they were afraid of getting stuck in the mud and being unable to take off again. At that time Pochala consisted of a few brick buildings and a broken pump from colonial days. It had been an administrative centre on the Ethiopia-Sudan border, marked by a river. The Anuak people, however, do not recognise this border as their land is on both sides of it. Before the refugees arrived no more than 100 families lived in the area with their cattle and millions of mosquitoes.

I will not easily forget the day we arrived. On landing we were greeted by more than ten thousand boys crowding around the plane coming to a standstill in the mud. Many of the boys were no more than ten years old, looking hungry, wondering whether we had brought any food. The only food we had were a few sandwiches, which the pilot had given to us before flying on to Lokichogio in Kenya, with the promise that he would collect us in a few days if it did not rain.

These boys had arrived the day before and they told us that many more would arrive that day. We greeted them and listened to them for hours. We could not do much more, with empty hands, than greet and welcome people as the bishop had suggested. Their leaders, who looked like a mixture of soldiers and teachers, told us that they had moved from the Fungido camp in the middle of a game park in Ethiopia. It was said that this camp had opened in 1987 to provide education for children from South Sudan. The boys had their copybooks still with them, but there were also guns lying around which I was not supposed to see. When we tried to talk to the boys, their leaders would answer instead, as if afraid that the boys would tell us the truth. When the boys themselves answered, they looked at the leaders for approval, as if they had been briefed what to say and what not to say. Wherever we walked or sat we were being watched. Thousands of boys stared at us. Only when darkness fell I secretly ate the sandwiches from the pilot. Bishop Taban gave me his sandwiches because he still had a few maize cobs, better than sandwiches he thinks.

35

The next day more returnees began to arrive. The only organisation present was the International Red Cross. They were assessing the situation and registering the returnees whilst we were shaking hands and listening to them. Listening, shaking hands and registering are all important of course, but I wonder. Listening is surely a priority. Each one of us was doing what they are best at. The Europeans were making plans and the Africans were building relations. The Red Cross had set up a small clinic but they only seemed to have aspirins and malaria tablets. But there is no medicine against hunger. There was no shelter for the boys. The only thing they happened to have was a mosquito net rigged on a few sticks, brought from Ethiopia. Luckily there were a few trees providing some shade.

I have often wondered what has become of all these boys since meeting them in Pochala more than ten years ago. Sr Sophie of Blessed Damian School, Kyatiri, told me that some of them were there. So last night I asked who was in Pochala in 1991.

Michael Deng put up his hand, but like the others he seemed a bit hesitant to talk about those times. This morning he brings me coffee in the guest house of Blessed Damian School, where he has joined the secondary section. I invite him to a cup of coffee and he accepts. Sr Sophie had told me that some boys were quite willing to talk about their lives, but not in a group. She had added that she might send someone, Deng as it turned out.

He is long and skinny, with a dark look in his eyes as if carrying the world on his shoulders. It takes a bit of time before we get really talking. His name Deng means that he is a Dinka, one of the biggest ethnic groups in Southern Sudan. It probably rained when he was born, because that is what Deng means. His full name is Deng Michael, or Mike, showing that he is a Christian. He has asked me not to take notes like the police and people in refugee registration offices. I put my notebook away. He is right, our talk should be more of a sharing than an interrogation.

I tell him that I come from Holland and that I have spent most of my life in Africa, between Kenya and Sudan. I ask him where he comes from. He mentions Bor, the birthplace of his father. Deng got excited when I told him that I have visited Bor, near the Nile, several times. I was there even after he left Sudan. We chat about his hometown, which he doesn't know. Even when you are no-where you must have come from somewhere.

Gradually we get talking and he starts reminiscing. He is a big man now, a lot taller than I am, but at the same time he seems almost shy and uncertain about his life, as if afraid of my disap-proval. His look appears darker than his skin when talking about his life. Now and then his face lights up with good memories.

The Dinka people live in Southern Sudan, in Bahr el Ghazal and part of Upper Nile. But Michael is a Dinka born in Khartoum, the capital, where his father worked, like a few million other peo-ple from the South. At least that is what his grandmother told him. He has no memories of Khartoum nor of his parents, but he thinks a lot about them.

His grandmother seems to be the first firm memory of his life. In 1982, when a little more than three years old, his parents took him to his grandmother in Marial Baai in the homeland of the Dinka people. His parents had decided that he should grow up in the rural area rather than in the slums of Khartoum, where most of the non-Arab people live. They must have thought that the boy would grow up among cows and in cattle camps near the Nile. At least that is Michael's guess, as he knows that parents want what is right for their children.

He remembers his life in Marial Baai with grandmother, who tried to be mother and father to him. There were also uncles and aunts, who looked after him as their own son. With other boys he herded goats and calves. When his parents took him to the rural area there was still a primary school in the village, where the chil-dren were taught in English and not in Arabic. His face betrays that his early youth in Marial Baai belongs to the good memories.

All that changed in 1983 when the civil war resumed in Sudan. It started in Bor, his father's hometown, when Dr John Garang de

Mabior rebelled against the Khartoum government. Perhaps it is more correct to say that Garang joined the rebellion that the government had asked him to put down. This Dr Garang, the leader of the SPLA to this day, is a Dinka like Michael Deng. Michael is proud to be a Dinka, like everybody else who is one.

But at this school in Uganda the Dinka are not popular, and Deng knows it. That is why he and others hesitated to talk in public last night. Many see the SPLA as a Dinka movement and quite a few, like Deng himself, have run away from the SPLA. Many feel that they have been victims of the SPLA, yet this same SPLA has often protected them, saved their lives and even tried to educate them.

When talking about this part of his life his face looks darker and sad. He does not remember the beginning of the war. For Michael bad memories start in 1987. He was not yet nine, and he had had no chance of going to school. It was a bad year. There was hunger in Bahr-el-Ghazal. Late in 1987 many people moved to Kordofan and Darfur but were not received with open arms by the government of Sudan which began to make use of hunger as a weapon against the people. In the past few years many people from South Sudan, in the hands of the SPLA then, had fled to Ethiopia. In 1987 165,000 of them lived in the three refugee camps of Itang, Dimma and Asosa. Deng did not know these figures, but we both read and heard about it later. But he does remember leaving his village in 1987.

The soldiers came and collected the boys to go to Ethiopia to give them an education; at least that is what they said. Like most boys in his village Deng was very keen on going to school. But not everybody was enthusiastic. His grandmother had tried to hide Deng, as she did not want him to leave, but she was badly beaten up. She was not the only one to be beaten. Some houses were burned down and cattle taken. When I ask whether SPLA soldiers had done this, Deng nods but adds that the *"murahileen,"* supported by the government in Khartoum, in others parts were even worse. They burned down whole villages, they took the cows, they took the grain, and they took the women and children as slaves. Deng is not sure, but thinks that grandma was killed in one of these raids.

Deng is not defending the SPLA but certainly does not want to blame the SPLA alone for this war. He seems disillusioned with adult society as a whole, with the government who killed his grandmother, with the SPLA who stole his childhood, with his guardians who promised education but sent him to the front.

He still remembers the name of Kuol Manyang, the commander who spoke to them at the beginning of the long journey. He spoke to them about education in Ethiopia and Deng wanted education. He was certainly willing to go to school, but it was his grandmother who did not want to let him go. "Commander Kuol Manyang told his subordinates to take us through the semi desert to this school in Ethiopia, so that one day South Sudan would have educated leaders," Deng tells me. I get the impression that Deng has a mixture of respect and fear for this Commander Kuol Manyang. The journey to Ethiopia started for Deng with more than two thousand boys. It must have been close to 1,500 km. through rugged terrain with no roads, partly savannah, partly bush and partly struggling through swamps. I recently flew over the area. Even from the air it seemed endless, too dry or too wet, with hardly any shelter.

Deng soon forgot about education, the journey was tough and long, dangerous and exhausting. He says now that they travelled more than 1,000 km., not far from my estimate of 1,500km. Even mixing up kilometers and miles, it really makes no difference. We often think in miles, but the people in Sudan think in days they have to walk to cover a distance. He knows that they walked for more than three months. They were lucky to find water to drink. They had taken some food from home but soon the only food they got was what was commandeered by their leaders from people along the way, who themselves often were hungry. The hunger was bad enough but also the wild animals seemed to be starving, and they fed on those boys who were too weak to get away. But the Murle people were worse than the lions. According to Deng, they saw the Dinka (or maybe the SPLA) as their enemy and they attacked the boys fiercely in Eastern Upper Nile before they could reach Ethiopia. Deng's was not the first group of southern Sudanese who tried to flee from the Sudan war to Ethiopia. Deng says: "We did not know the way to Ethiopia but we could find it by following the trail of bones of the people who had tried to get there before us but had died along the way." Of Deng's group also many died. Deng survived, although he does not know how. He suggests that it was all God's help. I let it pass and don't ask further, but I wonder why God did not help the others.

All this was happening in early 1989 when I had just arrived in Yambio in Western Equatoria. That part of southern Sudan is very fertile and seldom knows hunger. At that time Azande land was still in government's hands. This government spread terrible stories about the SPLA, portraying it as a Dinka movement to take over the south Sudan. In Yambio I first heard stories about child-soldiers in the SPLA army. I did not know what to believe, as it was obvious that, at that time, the Azande people certainly were not fans of the Dinka people or of the SPLA. Some people in Yambio seemed to hate the Dinka more than they hated the ruling Arabs, or possibly they were afraid to be liberated by the SPLA. There was a lot of propaganda against the SPLA; being liberated by them meant to be liberated from everything one possessed.

One day a Red Cross pilot landed in Yambio, where he had to stay the night with us because of bad weather. He had been in Ethiopia and confirmed that there were more than a quarter of a million Sudanese refugees in Ethiopia by April 1988. He also told me about a new camp in Fugnido, one of the game parks of Ethiopia, where thousands of very young boys looked more dead than alive when they arrived. This pilot thought that nearly half of them had died on the way, and that another 15% died soon after arrival. I use the word "child-soldiers," but the Red Cross personnel are usually very neutral and very vague. He certainly did not deny that there might be child-soldiers among them. It is now obvious to me that Deng was one of the boys who arrived in Fugnido more dead than alive.

I pour him another cup of coffee before I ask about his stay in Ethiopia. He pauses as if to think what to tell me and what not to tell me. There are no guardians here but even so it is not easy for Deng Mike to tell everything that happened to him. I try to make it easier for him by not asking too many questions and by not interrupting him.

His problems were not over as a refugee in Ethiopia. He had lost contact with his family, he had left his homeland and he thinks, probably rightly so, that only those who have gone through the experience themselves know what it is to be a refugee. One of his friends said later: "As refugees, we are victims of violence and war, we run for protection to other countries, but without homeland we are like tailless dogs."

Deng Mike tells me that in the beginning there was hardly any food and they had to live on what they could find in the bush, at times just leaves. Animals were aplenty. At times the soldiers were able to kill one, but more often the animals killed some boys.

"We had too many enemies at once," Deng says. "There was hunger, and many diseases like cholera, yellow fever, measles and scabies in the buttocks and under the fingernails. The local people were also enemies to us. We were like human beings without value. Malaria killed many, but there was no medicine till the International Committee of the Red Cross arrived. With the coming of the ICRC we felt free from hunger and disease, as we had food and medicine. There was also some schooling."

From Benjamin Madol, a priest who was with them, I hear that there were 12 schools, with double streams, each school catering for about 1,500 children, mainly boys. Radda Barnen, the Swedish Save the Children run by Ethiopians, supported the schools. The UN provided the food.

Deng must have been about ten at the time. But even with the arrival of the ICRC life had not become a paradise. In many ways the SPLA protected them, as teachers but also as military trainers.

The Churches were also very much present in these camps and at times the pastors cared for the boys together with the leaders of the SPLA. Deng tells me that the sisters of Mother Theresa were kind to the boys, especially when they were sick.

Here Deng was baptised and given the name Michael, the name of the guardian angel whose protection he needed badly at that time. Here they learned to use biblical images and songs to describe their journey and the hard life of refugee camps.

Deng talks about the hard work they had to do and which they could hardly manage as children. He explains that they did this to make them strong and he adds, "In the meantime they were 'culling' the children of the poor. One day we were sent with sixty boys to the bush to look for grass and long and short poles to build houses. The wild animals attacked us and only 15 of us returned not wounded or injured. Other boys died through anxiety, worrying about the cattle they had left behind when forced to go to Ethiopia. Again others were worried about the brothers and sisters they had left at home." I don't ask much; I just listen to Deng and wonder whether it is typical of a Dinka first to talk about the cattle and only later about parents, brothers and sisters. Deng talks quite openly now, somehow giving the impression that he wants the story to be known.

I still wonder whether they were child-soldiers but refrain from asking. But Deng tells me that after two years of this life, which was far from easy, he was taken with others for military training. They were grouped by age and taken to different places for training. He adds that a sufficient number of boys was always left in camp to attract food from the UN and other relief organisations. Some were taken for commando training to Bango "to be trained in all the tactics of war" as Deng puts it.

With them the SPLA wanted to create the *jesh ahmar* ("Red Army" in Arabic). These young Red Army soldiers were supposed to be the shock troops of the movement, very committed and loyal to the leadership of the SPLA. I have heard that in the early nineties there were close to 17,000 of these in Panyido. Deng himself, perhaps because he was still young, or not loyal enough, was sent to the military training field of Markaz, three hours walk from the camp. He tells me about the endless drilling and exercises which he considered too heavy for himself and his colleagues. He is also convinced that their trainers at times called an assembly when it started to rain just to take revenge for what they had to go through when they were trained themselves. When Michael talks about this time he looks rather miserable and he adds, "It was so painful that I felt sorry to be alive. I blamed my parents for getting married and giving birth to me. We were told to sing a song of praise about the rebel leader Dr John Garang de Mabior. Other boys tried but I was so miserable that I could not." It was a bad time, but still worse was to come. Deng sips some coffee before he tells me about the next chapter.

For many years the SPLA enjoyed the support of President Mengistu of Ethiopia, whom they were supporting against the different groups trying to overthrow him. That Mengistu was overthrown was a blessing for the people of Ethiopia but not for the many Sudanese refugees staying in that country. Michael Deng tells me how they were attacked by the Oromo rebels and how they fled with their leaders back to Sudan. Many were taken to the Nasir area but Michael's group fled towards Pochala. As they were fleeing they were bombed by government of Sudan planes; many died on the way, others lost the few belongings they had, as they had to cross rivers and many of those who could not swim drowned in the swamps.

In Pochala, Deng and I met for the first time, meaning really that we were both there for a few days in 1991. Deng does not remember my first visit, perhaps because we did not bring food. He only remembers that they had to wait long before food was brought. I myself will always remember how disappointed they looked when only people came out of the plane but no food or medicine was offloaded.

But two priests, Fr Dominic Matong and Fr Benjamin Madol, who had come with the boys from Ethiopia, were very happy to see us. They lived with the boys under the trees, they had a tent, but the boys had at the most a mosquito net. They sat under the trees with their copy books. Father Benjamin and Father Dominic had travelled with some of the boys from Rumbek and Wau. Father Dominic has died since; Fr Benjamin has told me a bit more of their story a short time ago. They accompanied the so-called "unaccompanied minors" but in some way they themselves could be called "unaccompanied priests." Benjamin was in Rumbek in 1986. The SPLA captured Rumbek but he stayed put. A few months later GOS recaptured Rumbek and Benjamin fled. He was in danger as he was seen as a collaborator with the SPLA and he thought it wiser to flee with the people. He disappeared travelling the same road as Deng, and part of the road they travelled together. Dominic fled about the same time from Wau. The Churches can get variously entangled in the war. In 1986 the bishop of Wau belonged to the Fertit people. The government mobilised and armed the Fertit to defeat the Dinka people. In such situations it is not always easy to know where the bishop stands and where the loyalties of the priests were. There was fear and distrust. Fr Matong was a Dinka whose tribesmen were being killed. He thought it better to disappear without telling his bishop where he was going. Dominic and Benjamin met in Ethiopia and together with some Episcopalian pastors they accompanied these minors, whilst they themselves had lost nearly all contact with the church at home. The Churches supported each other. After some time they were accepted by the Churches in Ethiopia. No, they did not convert the SPLA, but through their influence the Marxist jargon of the first years of the SPLA certainly decreased. They had their own compound where they cared for some of the more traumatised boys. The Churches worked closely together and the New Sudan Council of Churches was really conceived in these refugee camps in Ethiopia.

Deng and I are still talking in the guesthouse of Blessed Damian School when his friend, Dut, arrives. Deng tells me that Dut was also in Pochala and that perhaps he can tell me more. Dut claims to remember Bishop Taban's visit to them, not mine. In 1991 he was still young and all Europeans looked very much the same to him. He is willing to talk but not now, he has more important things to do. He has come to call Michael Deng to play football. Sports is not obligatory in the school, but it certainly is very popular among the students, an outlet for so much which otherwise would be suppressed. Dut agrees to meet me tomorrow.

Michael looks at me as if to ask whether this will do. I really still have a few questions I would like to ask but he shared quite a bit. What right do I have to ask more, I who have shared so little of my own life with Michael Deng? I thank him for his story, or part of the story. I thank him for his struggle, for not giving up.

Deng is not Michael's real name. Deng is a very common Dinka name. The story of Michael, with small changes here and there, is not only Michael's story but the story of thousands of Dinka boys and boys of other tribes. As many thousands or more cannot tell their own story anymore, having died in the war, Michael Deng has told their story today on their behalf. I have promised him to pass it on.

Lion-hearted Dut

*"Not only success should be praised,
but also the effort."*

(Ugandan proverb)

After classes Dut comes to see me. He is not in the least shy, as Deng was yesterday. Before I can ask him any question he has his own. Deng told him that I know Fr Benjamin Madol. Do I know where he is and why he has not come to visit him?, he asks. For several years and all the way from Ethiopia to the Kakuma camp in Kenya Fr Benjamin had been a father to him, and now he hasn't heard from him for several years.

Luckily I was in touch with Fr Benjamin. I had visited him not long before. I tell Dut that Fr Benjamin is parish priest in Yirol in Bahr el Ghazal, his home country. I agree with him that a father should visit his children, but the many boys to whom Fr Benjamin acted as father in Ethiopia, Sudan and Kenya, are now spread all over the world, even as far as the USA and Australia. Fr Benjamin cannot visit them all. Dut knows all that, but he does not find life easy without a father. Sr Sophie is a bit of a mother for him, but there are some matters he would have liked to discuss with Father Benjamin: he might even know where Dut's real parents are. I promise to get him at least the postal address. He wants to know everything about my recent visit to Bahr el Ghazal, I comply, but I

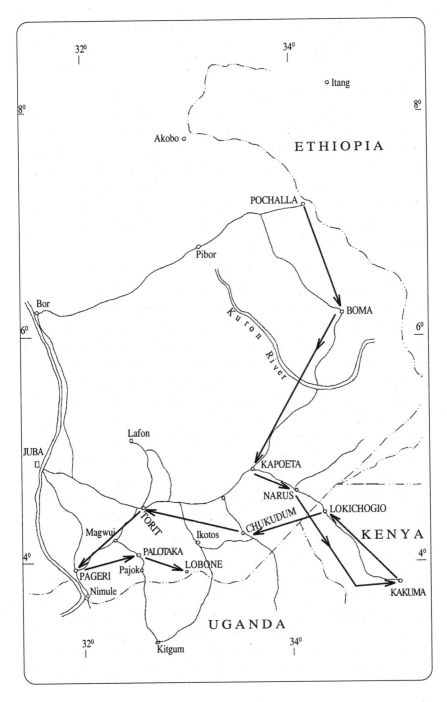

32⁰ · 34⁰ ·

ᵒ Itang

8⁰ 8⁰

Akobo ᵒ ETHIOPIA

POCHALLA ᵒ

ᵒ Pibor

Bor ᵒ *Kuron River*

6⁰ 6⁰ BOMA ᵒ

Lafon ᵒ

JUBA ᵒ KAPOETA

NARUS

Magwui ᵒ TORIT CHUKUDUM LOKICHOGIO

Ikotos KENYA

4⁰ 4⁰

PALOTAKA

PAGERI Pajok LOBONE KAKUMA ᵒ

Nimule

UGANDA

32⁰ · 34⁰ ·

Kitgum ᵒ

47

certainly don't know enough to still Dut's hunger for news from home. It takes time before Dut continues the story where Deng left off yesterday, under the trees in Pochala near Fr Benjamin's tent.

I have told him that I might use some of what he tells me to inform people about what he and others had to go through to get some education. I tell him that I will not use his own name, but he wants to know what I will call him. I ask what he would suggest, preferably a fairly common name among his people. There and then he chooses Dut. It means something like "strong-hearted," a name given to a newborn child when the child before him has died. I find it a fitting name, as many of his brothers with whom he had travelled to Ethiopia had died.

He remembers Pochala. They were not starving at the time of my visit, but life was not easy. In Ethiopia they enjoyed refugee status and the UNHCR had cared for them. In Pochala they were displaced people with no guarantee of any help. They were happy that the Red Cross had arrived and started registering people. What Dut remembers most of the first days in Pochala is the millions of mosquitoes. He had lost his mosquito net when fleeing from Ethiopia, and was lucky to find another boy willing to share his net with him. It took quite a bit of time to get relief organised for the many returnees. Dut remembers being hungry in Pochala. "At times we were so hungry that we felt like eating our fellow humans," he says. They would have liked to move on, but could not get through the swamps in the rainy season. And then by the time the food arrived and the situation had improved, the next enemy arrived.

Close to Christmas 1991 the local people of Pochala, the Anuak, with the help of Ethiopia and probably armed by the Sudan Government, started attacking them. Dut and other boys, led by some SPLA soldiers, tried to defend Pochala. It was his first experience as a soldier and he saw many around him shot. Dut was not afraid to shoot: "Kill or be killed," one of his trainers had told him. But they did not have enough guns and ammunition; the enemy was too strong. What could they do with a gun against tanks? Dut with more than 10,000 child-soldiers had to flee and run for their lives without being able to take much with them. He does not remember how long it took them to reach Kapoeta, but it was a long, very long, walk. He remembers arriving in Boma where the Red Cross welcomed them again and supplied food and water from then on. They were lucky that the dry season had started and they could walk through the dry Kuron river. In Kapoeta they would be safe, or so they were told. It was not the first time that things turned out to be different from what they had been promised.

Arriving in Kapoeta, tired, skinny and many of them sick, they should have had some rest to recover. But the war was escalating again between the government and the SPLA in Eastern Equatoria. Dut says, "Mobilisation started just when we thought we were safe. The whole of Eastern Equatoria was mobilised for enough forces to fight the attacking Arab forces." In 1992, during peace talks in Abuja, Kapoeta, a SPLA stronghold, fell to the government. So did Torit, taken back on 13th July after being under SPLA control for about three years.

From the end of 1990 Torit was my place of residence. The offices of the NSCC were located there, but I was in the Netherlands when Torit was taken by the government. I lost most of my belongings but I was safe. It was very different for the locals, who lost their homes once more, and many lost their lives. A new stream of 150,000 refugees got under way from Eastern Equatoria to Uganda. Dut was not among them, however. Once more he had the feeling that he was born in the wrong place or at the wrong time. Many returnees from Ethiopia, who were near Kapoeta coming from Pochala and Nasir, fled towards the Kenyan border. The arrival of the first 30,000 marked the beginning of the Kakuma refugee camp in the northern desert of Kenya. Among them were quite a few of the boys Dut had met in Ethiopia and Pochala. Dut, who had some fighting experience, was not allowed to settle in Kenya. He was recruited once more by the SPLA. He talks about this terrible time without showing much emotion. In matter-of-fact way he continues his story.

"We had to fight or be killed. We fought near Torit and even got close to Juba. One day we were completely defeated. Many of us were killed, and we were scattered in the bush where the rain washed us as it washed the animals. We lived like animals, and I tell you, we really became wild. Anything or anybody that crossed our path was killed. The only thing that could save us was our gun. For three days I was in the bush without meeting anybody. I did not sleep, but I collapsed on finally meeting my people again. In the end we were worn out by hunger, the cold and the rain."

As he tells me all this, I figure that at the time he could not have been more than 14. He goes on: "We were regrouped and had to go back to the battle field to collect the wounded and care for them. But the wounded enemy we had to finish off. They would ask for water, but we were told to kill them instantly as they were enemies." He looks at me as if expecting a disapproving head shake. He is right. I don't approve of killing a wounded enemy, but who am I to judge what Dut did when not even 14?

Then he thinks of what came next and his face lights up. He asks whether I know Commander William Nyon Bany. I did know him fairly well when we both lived in Torit in 1990-91. Did I know he had rebelled against the SPLA faction lead by Dr John Garang? Yes, I had heard about that also, and I had met him once in his Lafon stronghold. That rebellion caused confusion within the SPLA in East Equatoria, Dut tells me. The soldiers did not know anymore who was on which side. Dut was on neither side after all he had gone through, and just managed to escape from the front line. But he could not completely escape from the SPLA in an area under their control. He was lured back, with the promise of education, to go to Palotaka.

At the time when the colonial government left education very much to the missionaries, the Catholic mission station of Palotaka, founded by the Comboni missionaries, was a renowned educational centre. They had started it in 1939 with "The Vernacular Teacher Training School" also called "Karolo Lwanga VTTS." Here teachers were trained for the mission schools of Eastern Equatoria. The missionaries could run the schools because the colonial government paid the teachers. At independence in 1956, and more so in 1964 with all the missionaries expelled from Southern Sudan, this school system came to an end. Post-independence education was not too strong and illiteracy increased again during the war. As the SPLA took over most of rural Southern Sudan, the school system collapsed further. Many teachers on government salary, like most civil servants, fled to neighbouring countries where there was education and salaries in the refugee camps. The Churches tried to start bush schools, supplying textbooks and some teaching material, but they could not pay salaries except in one or two mission schools.

It cannot be said that the SPLA was not concerned about education; in the mid 1980s they sent hundreds of boys to Cuba via Ethiopia. This was not a great success. Some returned completely alienated from their own culture, only speaking Spanish. The UNHCR provided education in the refugee camps in Ethiopia, and Dut received some of that. But after the fall of Mengistu that chance vanished. The SPLA had received educational support in Ethiopia, and perhaps they were hoping to get it in South Sudan too. In 1991 they started the FACE (Friends of African Children's Education) Foundation.

Dut was one of the more than 1,000 children, mainly boys from different tribes, who went to Palotaka in the hope of continuing their education. He was able to join Primary School in class four in 1992. But the programme did not get much support, especially when the SPLA fell out with the local people when the soldiers, just before Christmas, began collecting the zinc sheets from their roofs for the school. Donors were hesitant to support the programme, afraid that it was a kind of military training camp.

Dut stayed only a few months in Palotaka. When Torit fell into the hands of the government in 1992, the war came too close and Palotaka was abandoned. Many children were taken to Moli Tukeru and later to Lobone, but gradually their numbers dwindled as many boys lost confidence in the scheme and fled. Dut was one of them. They fled to Pageri and later to the Aswa camp for the displaced. All he knew was that he wanted education and was not going back to the front.

As I listen to him it is obvious to me that we often underestimate the importance of education for the people of Southern Sudan. Many refugees now in Uganda, Ethiopia and Kenya did not flee only because of the dangers of the war, but also because they wanted education for their children or, in the case of Dut, for themselves. The world recognises the right to education for refugees but hardly anyone is willing to pay for the education of hundreds of thousands displaced people in Sudan.

After the failure of the FACE foundation Dut was sorry not to have fled earlier. He joined some friends who had fled to Kakuma in Kenya. He had heard that there were schools there, but it is not easy to get there from Aswa.

Unexpectedly he got help. One morning Commander Kuol Manyang Juk reappeared. He was the one who had promised education years earlier when Dut was on his way to Ethiopia. One day he visited the camp where Dut and many others were staying. I remember this commander well from my time in Torit in the early 1990s. At that time he was telling the Churches to do more for boys' education, he nearly ordered us. We hesitated, as we were afraid that all he wanted were trained recruits for his army. He still talked about education, and Dut, who had nothing to lose, decided to believe him. When Commander Kuol Manyang went to eastern Equatoria near the Kenya border Dut decided to go with him.

I regret not having taken notes, as I am losing track of some details. Dut had hope again. He describes it as "God rescuing him from the war and putting him again on the way to education." But it was not as simple as getting the bus fare from commander Kuol and taking the bus to Kenya. There were no roads and no buses. He talks about being in one place for 7 months, getting some education and then moving elsewhere. It could have been Labone. From there he went to Chukudum where he spent a full month secretly planning his escape to Kenya, confident that God was planning some good years for him after the seven meagre ones left behind. Just like many Sudanese refugees, Dut uses near-biblical language to describe his journey to Kenya, the Promised Land.

It was all very tricky. He could not escape without the help of the soldiers, since he was trying to hitch a lift on one of their lorries. It was important that they should not notice his attempt to escape. He knew they were going to Lokichogio and he hid in the lorry. On being discovered he pretended that he had to get some of the things of one of the commanders from the lorry. They left him alone and left, thinking he was going to Lokichogio on an errand for one of the commanders. He remembers that the vehicle stopped in Narus, where many people wanted to get onto the lorry. It was difficult to hold on to his place with grown-ups trying to displace him. He managed to stay on. Next stop was near the Kenyan border where the SPLA had a camp. He was relieved when the lorry started moving again and he knew that he was in that promised land, Kenya, where he would be free and where there was education.

But it is not at all simple to become a refugee in a neighbouring country. Dut was not received with open arms at the police and immigration office in Lokichogio. He tells how he and others were searched by the police, how these same policemen threw bullets among their luggage and then started accusing them of bringing weapons and ammunition into Kenya. I am not sure whether to believe Dut or the police. I know that there are refugees who smuggle weapons into Kenya, and I know that police can be cruel and unfriendly to refugees. Dut says: "They laughed at us and they beat some of us and said that we as refugees would suffer till the second coming of Christ from heaven, if there is going to be one." After that they were brought to the immigration office, where the officers did not treat them much better than the police had. Th got hardly any food and it took nearly a week to get registe·

refugees. They were free but not that much. They could not leave the compound.

Dut kept hoping that next step would mean the end of suffering. It looked like that when three Isuzu lorries arrived, sent by the Kakuma refugee camp manager. They travelled across the northern desert through Turkana country. The Turkana people, while related to the Sudanese Toposa, do not welcome all these refugees from Sudan. Every day they see lorries with relief food going to Lokichogio for the Sudanese and they themselves, who often also go hungry, don't get anything. Dut continues: "On arriving at Kakuma we drove to the UNHCR compound, where we were offloaded like stones that nobody cared about. We were kept there for two days with hardly any food, and without allowing us to enter the camp. Later on we heard that our two-day waiting was due to a tribal conflict raging in the camp. When we finally were let in I felt lost, for I did not know anyone. But people came to have a look at the new arrivals. One boy I had met in Ethiopia saw me and welcomed me. I could stay with him."

Dut remembers the date very well, 1st October 1993. He must have been about 15 when he became a refugee in Kenya. Kakuma, the refugee camp in the desert, 75 miles from the Sudan border, was not the paradise Dut had dreamed about and for which he had suffered so much. He describes the situation in the camp as a miniature South Sudan. People were suffering, blaming each other and quarrelling endlessly. Originally the camp had been started for Sudanese refugees, but now there were Somalis, Ugandans, Burundians, Ethiopians and Tanzanians. They, as refugees, brought the war with them. They would insult each other, or quarrel about a girl, whenever and wherever they gathered. One person would start beating another for no reason or out of pure frustration. Others would join in and a tribal mini-war would start with dead and wounded. There never seemed to be enough food. The land was a rainless desert, so people could not grow anything. Moreover they hardly dared leave the camp for fear of the Turkana. The only benefit the camp had brought to the Turkana seemed to be the clean drinking water from the boreholes sunk for the refugees. Dut did not like it. He worried and wanted to flee.

But his friend from Ethiopia had introduced him to one of the schools. It was one of the 21 primary and 3 secondary schools in the camp. Close to 25,000 children got some form of education in Kakuma. Such an opportunity was a reason for Dut to stay, after all education had been the reason for his long journey. He had to get used to the Kenya system of education, quite different from those of Ethiopia and Sudan. But the worst for Dut and the other pupils was that there were very few qualified teachers in both primary and secondary schools. Dut thinks that they were not paid well. For the many pupils there were not enough textbooks. One of the good things Dut remembers is that copybooks were free. He struggled hard and managed to finish his primary school in Kakuma. But the many problems did not allow him to get good marks. He got only 420 out of 750. It was not enough to be sponsored for a secondary school. But even with higher marks it would have been far from easy to get a sponsorship in Kenya, Dut explains. It was 1996.

He had heard that in Uganda there were more opportunities to be sponsored, as there were more government and non-governmental organisations supporting the Sudanese refugees. Dut's facts may not be 100% true, but I have heard them before from other sources and I am inclined to believe him. Dut wonders what next, but after considering all kinds of options he is more and more for giving up education in Kenya.

Even after opting for Uganda, he had to plan how to get there and pay for the journey. Dut phrases it his own way: "I entered a very deep thinking to plan and make my journey succeed with the help of God." He waited for the day of food distribution, collected his ration and sold it, but even that was not enough to pay for the journey. But he had found somebody willing to buy his refugee card. Refugee identity is worth quite a lot in Kenya and this card would not help Dut in Uganda.

· But even after the very deep thinking and getting some money, it was not a simple matter to leave the camp, certainly not without his refugee card. He was afraid of the Turkana and even more so of the Kenya Police who had abused and beaten him before. He managed to get to Lokichogio with Kenya public transport without much difficulty. There he spent two days hanging around for vehicles going to Sudan. He hardly ate as he had to save his money for transport, and it was too dangerous to go on foot, for the Toposa thought nothing of killing a boy just to get what little belongings he carried. Dut does not want to describe the journey from Lokichogio to Nimule, but it was not any easier than the journey from Aswa to Kakuma camp. It did not take as long because Dut had learned a few tricks since, not to get caught by the police, the SPLA or wild animals. Without a penny he arrived at the Uganda border, entering via Agoro. I am astonished at how Dut remembers the names of all these small places. I have difficulty in finding them on any map. He was received better than in Kenya, or maybe he was a bit wiser and had no bullets in his luggage. In Agoro he inquired carefully about the different camps in Uganda before he went on to Kitgum to have himself registered as refugee in Uganda. The journey was somehow alright, he tells me, difficult but not unmanageable.

He was glad to be in Uganda but it was hard to get used to the new place. He had to adjust to a new climate, with rain and cold. He also had to get used to different people yet again. He continues: "I got sick with a sickness unknown to me. I got completely demoralised and confused when I saw the insecurity in the north of Uganda. I was afraid and I asked myself why I had run away from trouble only to get into more trouble. Or was the whole world one single trouble? I asked God why he made me suffer like that, what had I done to the world. I cried all night when going to bed and woke up without a solution. Why was I alone, separated from my parents? Was this God's plan, or the devil's? I had no news of my parents, of where they were. I felt like an orphan, alone in the world and sorry to be alive." With these words Dut pictured how traumatised and depressed he really was as a newly arrived refugee in Uganda. Listening to what he had been through, I was astonished at his not having collapsed earlier, but I was even more astonished at what the people of Sudan have been able to endure without giving up hope.

The horrible stories about the Lord's Resistance Army in the north of Uganda made him even more afraid, but also reminded him of what he had gone through fighting at the front himself. When I try to inquire about the LRA he avoids answering, as if that was not his business or he did not want to accuse others. He suggests that I ask one of the other pupils in the school who fled from the Lord's Resistance army and who knows more about it than he does.

Dut ended up in Achol-Pii refugee camp. It had its problems: with the rainy climate one needed better shelter. He tells me how he had to run not to be shot by a drunken soldier. The dispensary was attacked by the LRA but they only took medicine and luckily did not kill anyone. AVSI, an aid organisation of the Italian bishops' conference, provided food, and the climate allowed people to grow some food. All that help made refugee life bearable, but what attracted Dut most was the school which he joined at primary level in Class Seven.

In Uganda they look down on Kenyan education, but that was not the reason why Dut joined a Ugandan school. Only those pupils who had been to school in a camp in Uganda could get a sponsorship for further education. Dut accepted the conditions and got on with his studies. This was not always easy with the insecurity around. He had not healed yet from the disease described earlier and felt very insecure. He did not have much confidence in himself anymore.

At the mock examination Dut got very high marks. It was a great boost. He recovered some self-confidence and trusted that he could pass the Primary Leaving Examination (PLE) of the Uganda National Examination Board (UNEB). He repeats these names for me to make sure that I get them correct and realise their importance. He studied hard for three months. The examination papers were brought; Dut sat the exam and was confident he had passed. This was 1998. Immediately after it, Dut fell sick for more than a month without being able to enjoy Christmas in the Achol-Pii refugee camp. He pauses a moment and then almost solemnly he goes on: "By luck, no, not luck but by God's plan I got cured. Then I received the good results of my examination." I am impressed. I tell him that after all that struggle he had passed primary school when he was nearly twenty. He looked pleased with himself, but the struggle was by no means over.

He went to fill in all the forms for sponsorship, but Dut found that the relatives of people in charge of the sponsorship board seemed to get preference. Dut knew that his marks were good. He did not give up, he had struggled too long to give up. He kept searching and somebody of the World Food Programme suggested Blessed Damian School. He knew that Bishop Taban and the Sisters had started a secondary school and that they had a soft spot for Sudanese children who had been struggling for education during the war.

Secondary education is important to Dut. But what is more important is that here he feels safe. There is no SPLA who might drag him back to the war, there is no Lord's Resistance Army to attack, and there are no police or immigration officers to abuse him. Blessed Damian is not only a school for Dut, but also a home. Sr Sophie is like a mother to him, and now that he knows Fr Benjamin to be in Yirol he will write to him. From his own parents he has not heard anything since leaving home in the late 1980s.

I ask him whether he wants to go back to Sudan. He has to think before answering. Of course he wants to go back, who doesn't want to go home? He knows that there is no place like home but he adds: "Only when there is true peace." By the way he says this it is clear that for Dut peace means more than signing a peace agreement, which is only a starting point for peace.

Without Education
We Shall Remain Slaves

"When the child asked,
'How do you hold the shield?'
The father answered,
'The shield itself will teach you, in war'."

(Akan proverb)

J met Commander Yousif Kuwa for the first time in 1993. He was the leader of the SPLA in the Nuba Mountains. We met in Nimule near the Ugandan border, far away from both our homes. I will not easily forget this impressive man, whose name I had heard before. He came to visit Bishop Taban together with other SPLA commanders. The bishop had made Nimule his base after fleeing from Torit when it was recaptured by the government in 1992.

Most of these SPLA commanders looked big and fierce in battle dress. But Yousif Kuwa, whom I had also imagined to be a fierce big guerrilla fighter, did not fit this image. He had a kind and gentle face, and he was smaller than I had expected a Nuba to be. Maybe he looked smaller because the other commanders were Dinka and Nuer people, who are very tall. There was something gentle and gentlemanlike about him. Even the army uniform did not make a real soldier out of him.

I was also visiting Bishop Taban in Nimule. Yousif and I happened to sit next to each other as we were drinking tea. It was easy talking to him. He asked me what I was doing in this part of the world. His question was not a formality; he really wanted to know. I told him I was working with Bishop Taban for the New Sudan Council of Churches. Although Yousif was a Muslim, he was well informed about the Churches and grateful for what the Council of Churches was doing for the people of Southern Sudan. He told me that Bishop Taban was a good friend of his, which was obvious to me from the way they had embraced and laughed together on the commander's arrival.

Commander Yousif expressed regret at my not having visited his native Nuba Mountains, that part of Sudan ethnically African but geographically belonging to the Arab North. Like most of his people he is a Muslim, but the Arabs could never convince him to be an Arab also. Yousif thinks that they tried to make Arabs of the Nuba people by imposing Islam, by making Arabic the medium of education and forbidding them to speak their own language in school. He was born a Muslim, but in matters of religion he calls himself a bit of a free-thinker. He feels that in many ways he is also a Christian, but above all he has largely an African spirituality. He is proud of being African, but even more of being a Nuba, in the same way as the Dutch feel more Dutch than European. He tells me that African history is ignored in the Arab schools. He only read outside school of how his forefathers established the Kush Kingdom and other great civilisations. He, a Muslim, explains that many of the Nuba people are Muslims but live in peace with Christians and the followers of African traditional religions. He did not fall for the government propaganda that the war was against Islam. Most of the SPLA leaders in the Nuba Mountains were Muslims like him. The first *jihad* (holy war) was declared on the Nuba people. He tells me that the government Muslim forces even burned down mosques in the Nuba Mountains. He knows that religion can be abused.

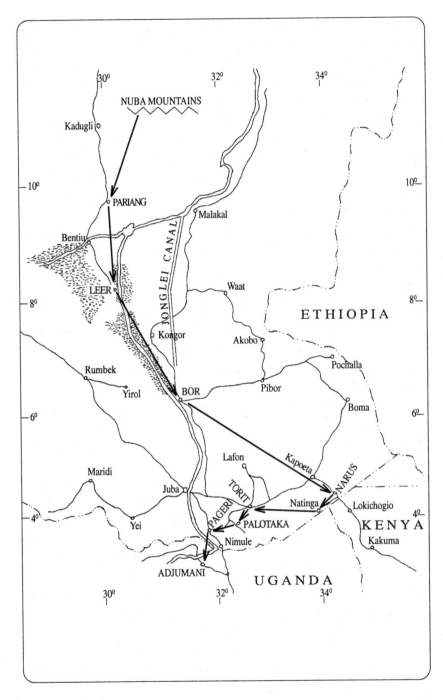

Over a second cup of tea, Yousif Kuwa Mekki asked me whether the New Sudan Council of Churches could not do more for education, as the missionaries had done in the past. What was wrong with the missionaries these days, he wondered. I try to explain that in the colonial days government not only supplied the greater part of the funds for the mission schools, but even paid the teachers. Yousif, who himself taught for seven years, knew that this was no longer so. Also many donor organisations hesitate to invest in education in Sudan as long as the war is on. He had hoped to find education for the Nuba boys in the so-called liberated areas. Education is important to him, but he thinks that his people and the boys feel that he has let them down. I know that we have no funds for education and remain non-committal, but this commander does not give up.

In a gentle but very convincing tone he starts to explain to me that without education the Africans in Sudan will remain *abid*, slaves. His people, the Nuba, know this better than other Sudanese. They are an African people living in the North. The Arabs referred to them as slaves, and often they were the ones singled out for the most debasing jobs like collecting human refuse. But they are courageous people who in colonial times could find a military assignment if they did not want to be domestic servants. When he was a young pupil the Arab teachers from the North did not want to teach them. "Why should future house boys be taught?" they asked. That is when Yousif started to rebel, and to struggle for his own education and that of the Nuba people. Most of his education he got in the north of Sudan. He came to know the Arabs very well, learning their ways and some of their tricks. He knows that they still try to keep Africans uneducated so as to suppress them more easily. When he was a teacher he thought a lot about this and in the end he went back to university to study political and social science. Through education he came to understand better how the Sudanese Africans were being discriminated against. Having learned their political games he was able to defeat some Arab politicians at the elections, thus becoming the political leader of the Nuba people. He fought for a different Sudan, where the many different identities would be respected. He was one of the first Nuba leaders to join the SPLA, which also claimed to fight for a new Sudan.

He had heard that the New Sudan Council of Churches is involved in training church leaders. He hears all this talk about "capacity building" but according to him it all starts with a good primary education: even the future soldiers should have a good basic education. I am a bit hesitant to start an argument with this Nuba leader who sounds so genuine and knowledgeable. In many ways I agree with him. I wished that we could get funds for basic education in Southern Sudan so that people didn't have to flee any longer to neighbouring countries to get their children educated. But I have also heard stories about the SPLA's collecting boys from schools and using them as child-soldiers. Even the name of this friendly commander has been mentioned in this context. I am inclined to believe this man who seems genuinely concerned about education. I risk asking whether he brought the many boys all the way from the Nuba Mountains to train them as soldiers or to give them some education. He answers with a further question: "Don't we also need educated soldiers?" I don't know what to answer. I certainly have no solution to offer on how to provide education for the many thousands of Nuba boys who have come to the South looking for education.

Perhaps I am lucky that the SPLA delegation has to leave to visit the hospital with the bishop. The last advice I get from commander Kuwa is: "Read the books of Julius Nyerere, a true African leader and teacher who knows the value of education." Education was for Commander Yousif Kuwa not only formal. "Life is a school, and one with great lessons," he said.

Yousif Kuwa Mekki died March 31st 2001. He is not only remembered in the Nuba Mountains but also at the Blessed Damian School in Uganda, where the first students were 56 Nuba boys. Quite a few of them are still around, especially in the secondary school section.

Last night I talked to one of them, taking notes as he spoke. He must have told the others, because this morning several came asking me to write their story too, so that the world may know about the suffering of the Nuba people.

They talk with love about the good fertile land of their country, good for cattle and crops. Jakob tells me that before this war they never needed relief. As many as 99 different tribes live there. Another corrects him, saying that they now are 100, as the Uduk people also live on the Nuba Mountains. Each tribe has its own dialect, traditions and even religion. They are adamant that they lived in peace before this government started manipulating religion and ethnic differences in the late 1980s. It is obvious that they are proud of who they are. Alalo says: "We are tough people, we are rocks, like St Peter in the Bible."

They seem to soften when I ask: "What do you miss most from home?" There is a silence as if I had asked an indecent question. They look at each other. In the end Aljou says: "Can you imagine not having seen your parents for more than twelve years? Can you imagine still remembering a few names of your siblings but even with closed eyes and trying hard not remembering what they look like?" I dare not say that I can imagine what it means, because only those who have experienced such a thing know what it means. Rather than asking more "stupid" questions I go back to the stories of struggle and suffering which they want the world to know.

I don't disagree with them. That's my idea too. I propose to give them a copybook and a pen to write down the story about their former life, how they survived and how they got here. They all accept the copybook and some start writing. A few days later we meet again and I get to hear something of the plight of the Nuba boys in this war. As I listen, my memories go back to my meeting Yousif Kuwa in Nimule in 1993. His name keeps coming up in the boys' stories.

Aljou writes almost solemnly: "Once upon a time, when I was nine, the chief of my village called all the men together on behalf of the governor of Southern Kordofan, Yusuf Kuwa Mekki. The head man was chairing the meeting, which was for men only. It was decided that all the boys between eight and fifteen must go to school for the future well-being of the Nuba people. Without education our people would become illiterate again. The governor instructed the people to set aside all the boys between eight and fifteen who were to go to school and prepare food for the long journey to Southern Sudan where they would get education. The whole village contributed. We received the blessing to go to school from our parents, and a week later we left."

Another boy tells me that that "Once upon a time" of Aljou was 1990, which he knows about as he was there too. In 1989 a great part of the Nuba Mountains fell to the SPLA. Yousif Kuwa became governor of the SPLA held area. This campaign for education was not only organised in Aljou's village but all over the Nuba Mountains under SPLA control. Not everybody was enthusiastic. Some mothers tried to hide their sons, but the exercise was not really voluntary either, for such mothers were badly beaten by the soldiers. At the same time it must be said that many boys were keen on schooling, although they had no idea of what was ahead of them. How many boys went is not clear to me; "very many" I am told by several boys. Nobody seems to know exact figures. They were in the thousands.

Aljou, now less solemnly, goes on, pointing out that there was no transport to take them to this school in Southern Sudan. They, and he was only nine, had to journey on foot. More than a thousand boys accompanied by teachers and protected by some soldiers travelled one and a half months to reach Ler in the country of the Nuer. Many boys died on the way of hunger and thirst. Aljou, at his young age saw them die. But not only hunger and thirst killed them. They were also ambushed by GOS troops and they were all scattered. It took time before they regrouped and some were never seen again. Maybe they died in the bush, maybe they were taken as slaves by the soldiers who ambushed them. Aljou does not know.

Another boy, Peter Kalo, remembers how sick he was on reaching lake Abeyad. He could not walk any more. There was no medicine, but he was carried to Fariyang by some of the older boys and by the soldiers who accompanied them. Here, in Fariang, he was left with the Dinka people. He could speak some Arabic, but most of these people did not understand either Arabic or the Nuba language. Just imagine a boy of ten, sick and miserable, left with strange people, with whom he cannot even speak. But these people seemed to care. They communicated without many words. He stayed there for two months and recovered somewhat. He was picked up by the next group of children on their way to education somewhere in the South.

Aljou had been happy to arrive in Ler, in the Upper Nile province, hoping to rest a bit and have some good food. But they were not welcome; there was cholera in Ler and many people had died. They were told to leave at once, they could not even spend one night there. He could not understand what it was all about but he had the feeling that they were being chased away. He found the Nuer people unfriendly despite their being under the same SPLA. He did not know that endless streams of displaced had passed through Ler before, on their way to Ethiopia.

Now he thinks that they were lucky to be chased away, because they did not contract cholera, and not only that. They were told that if they rushed to the Nile, which was not far, they might be able to catch the boat to Bor. They did rush, just in time for the soldiers to stop the boat from leaving as many of the smaller boys had not yet arrived. They spent the night on the banks of the Nile. Aljou remembers that that night one of his friends died, just before embarking. I believe him when he says that life is miserable when you are young and have to look on when your friend dies. I ask him whether this was the first time he saw someone die. He had seen many die on the way, but this was his friend and that made it a lot more painful.

There were too many boys for the boat to take them all. The soldiers selected the younger and the weaker ones. For once Aljou was happy to be considered young and weak. In the morning he embarked with other young and weak boys. The older and strong ones had to walk through the desert. The boat took them to Bor in Dinka land. There they stayed for two weeks to recover from their long journey. There was food, and the Dinka people even slaughtered cows for them. Aljou is not the only one with good memories of the reception in Bor. Alalo Patrick, who is biblically inclined, says it was like the multiplication of bread in Mt 14:13-21: the people of Bor shared what they had and there was enough for all. Maybe the true miracle is that they survived because so often the people on the way shared the little they had.

At first they waited for the older and stronger ones to arrive, but the soldiers thought it better to move on walking to Torit. He thinks it was towards the end of 1990 or was it already 1991? He is not quite sure. It doesn't really matter.

In 1990 I had also come to Torit for the first time. I remember large groups of boys sitting along the road near the school just outside town. Their leaders did not look like soldiers to me. But so many displaced passed through Torit at that time that I was a bit afraid to stop and ask. They might have asked for food again. At that time the NSCC, just starting, had very little to give. And I had not yet learned that when you have nothing to give, you can at least shake people's hands or lend them a listening ear. Had I taken the trouble to stop and listen, I might have met Aljou or Alalo Patrick in 1990. In Torit they waited for the older and stronger ones to arrive.

These older and strong ones were less strong after their long walk, but still strong enough to be selected for military training upon arrival. Were they cheated out of their education and brought to the South only to be trained as soldiers, or was the SPLA forced to recruit them by the escalating war? When asking that question in the past, I was told that people give different answers depending on whether they talk during the day or at night. As a non-Sudanese I usually hear only what is said by day. Moreover I have also learned that both answers can be true.

Both Aljou and Alalo were considered too young for military training. They were sent to school in Palotaka, which had at least 1,000 boys. This school of the FACE Foundation certainly did offer some military training. The Nuba boys did not find it easy to be with boys of so many different tribes. There were Dinka, Nuer, Lutuko, Acholi and so many others they cannot remember. Aljou remembers that the Nuer treated them badly and that the Dinka gave them enough to eat when they walked through their land. Aljou, still looking forward to education, found Palotaka a bit too much for his age. In the morning they underwent military drill. Then they schooled all day and in the evening they had to work in the extensive school gardens. They had to build shelters against the bombing Antonov aircraft and very soon the food was finished. Even the cattle were dying. Only the jiggers seemed to increase all the time, making it difficult for those boys to walk. He remembers that Bishop Taban and Father John Gary took pity on them and gave them some food.

But soon enough things got worse due to "insecurity in the Torit area" as Alalo puts it. When Torit fell, Palotaka was no longer a safe place. They moved on to Moli Tukeru. But that did not last long either. They travelled on to Natinga where, according to Alalo, there were 8,000 boys. Those who had not moved on because of the insecurity were in the end chased away by the jiggers.

Again they had to face a selection for military training. There was no escaping. It did not mean that Aljou felt, or was, stronger than the year before. He thinks that the soldiers changed the rules for selection. He says that this time they were trained in groups of only young ones. He explains the rationale, but I am not sure whether he discovered this at the time or whether he thought it over in the safety of Uganda. He puts it as follows:

"It was because the young don't fear anything when fighting. One day we went to attack a stronghold of people who had rebelled against the SPLA mainstream. When we arrived we did not know that they were expecting us and were ready to face us. We were ambushed and we were badly beaten, many were killed. God was good enough to protect my life because my rifle had very many bullets. We called it the "forty six", I don't know its real name, otherwise I would tell you. I fired and fired, I gave them a hard time until the grass caught fire, as it was the dry season. They ran away before the fire, I escaped and my life was saved."

Aljou thinks this was 1994, the year when many of his comrades, as he calls them, ran away and only a few of them were left. He kept count of the battles. The fourteenth was a tough one. He remembers it well: "We fought one whole week without rest against the Arabs at a place called Pageri near the Ugandan border. The Arabs had said that if they overtook that place they would continue to the border and even finish off the Ugandans. People died like animals on both sides. We did not have time to dig trenches but one could take the body of a dead comrade or a dead Arab enemy and put them in the form of stones or a trench to protect oneself. We knew that bullets would not penetrate a dead body and so the dead protected us." Again he survived and he fled with his gun.

In June 1994 he and some others with whom he had come from the Nuba Mountains travelled up to Narus, to side with one of the commanders. Aljou does not name this commander but other boys, like Alalo Patrick, tell me that this commander was Yousif Kuwa Mekki.

When soldiers were mobilised again to attack Torit, Yousif Kuwa thought that Aljou was too young, or that he needed a rest. He was not sent to the war but the commander in Narus made him one of his bodyguards or at times sent him to guard a roadblock. That is where several of the boys came to know Bishop Taban who also lived in Narus. He always talked to them when they stopped him at a roadblock. Aljou says: "When this bishop saw us suffering in the bush and heard that we were from the Nuba Mountains he took pity on us." Some remember getting a lift from the bishop from Narus to Chukudum where the bishop and Commander Kuwa talked.

I know that Commander Kuwa and the bishop talked more than once about education. Commander Kuwa had promised his people that he would get education for their sons in Southern Sudan. But with the constant fight between the SPLA and the GOS there was not much time for learning. They had only learned how to survive in a war zone. Yousif Kuwa pleaded once more with Bishop Taban to see whether he could do something for the education of at least some of the Nuba boys who were in his diocese. Might not it be better to take them to Uganda where there was no fear of SPLA recruitment?

The bishop was probably more understanding than I was when meeting Yousif Kuwa in Nimule in 1993. Education in Sudan at that time was too complicated and they decided that Uganda might be a better place. In Uganda the boys did not have to worry about being picked up again to be sent to the frontline. These boys were far from home and there were no parents to protect them when some commander or other decided again that he needed more recruits.

The bishop knows that the parents, especially the mothers, can play an important role in these matters. Some years ago Bishop Taban started a school for girls in Narus. For many of the displaced and also for many people in SRRA a school for boys seemed a greater priority than one for girls. They kept asking for a boys' school. The bishop pointed out that he had no guarantees that the SPLA would not come and take the boys as recruits for the army. But when the parents kept asking for a boys' school and the SPLA promised that they would not interfere, a boys' school was started. The parents were very much involved and that made a difference.

70

For a few years the school went well and the SPLA kept their promise, but they still had a *kasha* to get new recruits. They came to school, rounded up the older boys and beat up protesting teachers. The parents complained to the bishop. He listened but pointed out that they had wanted the school and that it was their own sons who had been taken. They got the message and held meetings to see what to do.

The mothers went to the barracks where their sons were kept and asked to see the commander in charge. They had suckling babies at their breasts. They asked the commander to let the boys go back to school and reminded him of the promise to leave the boys alone and not to interfere with their education. He told them that this was an emergency and that they should be proud of letting their sons serve in the army of the SPLA. He wanted to dismiss them. Women should not interfere in matters of war. But it was not so simple as he had thought. One woman with a baby at her breast stood up an said: "If you think that we only give birth to our children to provide the SPLA with soldiers, why should we suckle them, why should we feed and care for them till you think they are old enough to take a gun? If this is your attitude take our babies now and suckle and feed them yourself." She put her baby at the feet of the commander and invited the other mothers to do the same. The soldiers pleaded with her to take their screaming babies. But they insisted that they would take their babies home only if their sons went back to school. The mothers won and the boys went back.

This happened four or five years after the bishop and Commander Kuwa were talking together about education for the Nuba boys. They were talking not only about Aljou or Alalo Patrick but in the end Bishop Taban went with 56 Nuba boys to Uganda in 1995. They arrived first in Adjumani where they were left in the care of Sr Sophie. It is easy enough to take the decision to educate boys from the Nuba Mountains, but more difficult to put it into practice. Moreover, the UNHCR was very hesitant to cooperate as they wanted the boys to stay in the refugee camp. There was even talk of starting an orphanage, but Sr Sophie and the bishop were adamant that these boys were not orphans but boys who for years had been on their way hoping to get education.

Aljou remembers very well spending one year in Adjumani without schooling. But Sr Sophie kept telling them that the bishop was working on a plan. Apart from not schooling they were looked after very well. They got blankets and food from the WFP; they even got toothbrushes. But what they really wanted was education. After waiting for nearly a year they were told that Bishop Taban and the Sisters had prepared a place for them near Masindi. This time it would be education.

Aljou is not the only one to remember the exact date, 4th November 1996. It was a day to remember. As the roads were unsafe because of the many attacks of the LRA, the UN provided a plane and the Nuba boys had their first experience of flying. They were flown from Adjumani to Masindi. But they were not exactly welcomed in Masindi. They had refugee papers, but the Ugandan police thought that refugees should be kept in refugee camps, knowing that there was no refugee camp in Kyatiri near Masindi. On telling the police that it was not a refugee camp but a school, started by the bishop and the sisters, they got into more trouble. They were all arrested while the aircraft flew back to bring the second group. They were even imprisoned for a few hours but they were not too afraid because the bishop and sisters were with them, and they remained calm. In the end all was sorted out and at exactly 5 p.m. they were released and brought to Kyatiri.

Compared to what it is today, the place was very bushy then. There were a few prefabricated buildings serving as a house for the sisters, a few classrooms and a dormitory. The Nuba boys found not just a school there but also a home, and many other boys also. That is my conclusion after listening to them. The first three Nuba boys have finished secondary school in Blessed Damian. They have returned to the Nuba Mountains with letters and messages from the others who haven't heard yet of their arrival. Aljou and a few others I am talking to hope to get a chance for further education here in Uganda before going back to the Nuba Mountains. Educated leaders are going to play an important role when peace comes to the Nuba Mountains. I ask what they want to study. Aljou wants to be a civil engineer like Amuka, who has put up most of the buildings in this school. Kanyitha hopes to be a medical doctor. But Alalo is convinced that today political science is just as important as in the days of Yousif Kuwa to keep the peace in the Nuba Mountains. As we talk there are peace talks for Sudan taking place in Kenya, or at least talks about a protocol for peace. These young men are sceptical about it all, but not without hope. They can't afford the luxury of giving up hope.

Aljou and the others know that I work in Sudan. They know that I knew Commander Yousif Kuwa Mekki whom they admire as their patron together with Bishop Taban. They really want to know whether I have been in the Nuba Mountains. I admit that I haven't, but that I hope to go there one day. One says: "We will meet you there," and then it is clear to me that the Nuba Mountains is their real home. Being a long way and a long time from home has not changed that. In Uganda they will remain foreigners; it is said in Africa: "A stump that stays in a river for a hundred years does not become a crocodile."

A Victorious Deserter

*"When you are running away
from your enemies in time of war
you do not wear a scabbard of bells."*

(Ewe proverb)

He stands there, watching from a distance, when I take a photograph of a few boys pointing out their Sudan homes on a map. The map has been painted on the wall of a school building of Blessed Damian School. I ask him where he comes from and he says he does not come from Sudan, his home is in the north of Uganda. When I ask him to indicate his home on the map, which also covers the north of Uganda, he does not do that, he only says: "Near Kitgum" and he walks away as if he did not want more questions.

A few days later I meet him again near my room in the guesthouse of the school. Here there are no Sudanese around. He seems more willing to talk. The school caters not only for war children from Sudan but also for victims of the war in Northern Uganda. This at times creates tension; in the war zone in Sudan boys captured by the LRA and Sudanese child-soldiers often fought each other. It is easy to call Ugandan boys who were abducted by the LRA "victims of the war", but a few years ago the Sudanese boys only knew them as enemies and vice versa. Listening to their stories I get the impression that the ex-LRA soldiers have more fighting experience.

We first talk about what we both know: the weather, the mosquitoes, the school having grown fast since my last being here and other subjects which keep the conversation going without giving too much away.

He tells me his name, Victor Onweng, an Acholi name. I tell him my name and explain that I am from the Netherlands but that I worked for many years in south Sudan. He seems to know all about me; Sr Sophie usually explains who the visitors are. They don't have to worry about strange faces. She told them that I was interested in their earlier life before coming to the school. But I have been in Sudan, therefore Victor is not so sure whether I am also interested in Uganda.

After a slow start, I ask him whether he knows that his name, Victor, means winner. He smiles and says that this is true in this school, after being a loser for several years. I don't understand. I ask him to explain further. We are sitting on the veranda of Father le Vacher, the school chaplain.

On inquiring with Deng a few days ago about the LRA, he suggested asking one of the boys in the school who had been with the LRA. Victor is one. He tells me what he knows and I tell him what I have heard.

Since independence in 1962, fertile and beautiful Uganda has had a number of presidents, rising to power mostly by military coup. Amin, the best known, came from the North as did most of the others. The Acholi people often held high rank in the army and therefore they had quite a bit of influence in the country. All that changed in 1986 when the military junta of Tito Okello was ousted by Museveni, who has been in power ever since. It is not easy to play the part of the loser in any war, but less so in Africa where the ousted ones conspire to oust the incumbents. The Acholi suffered for being seen as the followers of the former leaders. Many of the soldiers could only go home and start farming again. They took it as a humiliation, apart from the fact that small farmers haven't got much of a chance when the economy is ruined. Somebody called the story of the LRA the story of the losers in Uganda. The Acholi people were losers when Museveni came to power in 1986. In many places he received a great welcome. But not in northern and eastern Uganda, where there was much mutual suspicion between the National Resistance Movement/Army and the former followers of Okello. The Acholi people felt that the new government wanted to destroy them militarily, socially, culturally and economically. The new administration was afraid and hostile towards the North, looking upon the people as enemies. Mutual suspicion and opposition grew. There were enough arms around to turn the opposition into an armed resistance.

Gradually an Acholi resistance movement grew. In the beginning it was called Uganda People's Democratic Army (UPDA) and later the Holy Spirit Movement (HSM), led by a woman called Alice Lakwena. She was a kind of prophetess who wanted to give back to the Acholi people their self-respect. She would anoint her followers with a special oil called *Mooya*, claiming that it would make them "bullet proof." Desperate people tend to do desperate things and many Acholi joined Alice Lakwena in her struggle to overthrow President Museveni. In 1987 her followers were certainly not bullet proof. They were badly defeated near Jinja and she fled to Kenya where, I believe, she lives to this day.

But all that was before the time of Victor, about which I probably know more than he does. For Victor the Lord's Resistance Army is the army of Joseph Kony, relative and disciple of Alice Lakwena, who continued her struggle against the government of Uganda after she fled to Kenya.

Joseph Kony was born in 1961 in a village called Adek, in the north of Uganda not far from Gulu. It is said that he was baptised a Catholic but he came from a family of witchdoctors. It is not clear at what time he began thinking of himself as endowed with supernatural powers. Now he is the leader of the LRA. This rebel leader claims that God has chosen him to be the new president of Uganda, and that is what the LRA is about. This army recruits mainly children by abducting them, often binding and brainwashing them with semi-religious rituals. Those who have called the LRA an army of children forget that the children who did not escape or die have grown up in that army, knowing nothing except guerrilla warfare.

Human rights groups, Amnesty International and UNICEF have written reports, charging that children not even ten years old are kidnapped, tortured, raped and virtually enslaved, sometimes killed, and all that in the name of the "Holy Spirit." The children are forced to take part in combat, carrying heavy loads and acting as personal servants to the rebels. I have heard about it. Victor has not only heard but experienced it himself. The story of when he felt he was not a winner slowly unfolds.

Since early youth, Victor lived in constant fear of the LRA in a village near Kitgum, in the north of Uganda not far from the Sudan border. He had a sister and three brothers, he tells me. His parents wanted him to go to school, and he wanted too. He had been told that without education there is no future, so he went to school in his village. Going to school in the north of Uganda is not as simple as it sounds. School fees have to be paid, and often one has to walk long distances. While true for many parts of Africa, here in the north of Uganda the LRA often attacks villages and communities. Schools are attacked and children abducted and taken to the camps of Joseph Kony in Sudan. There Kony enjoys the protection of the Sudan government which claimed, probably rightly, that Museveni supported the SPLA. The GOS supplied them with weapons. In return the LRA supported the GOS in its war against the SPLA, or they attacked the Sudanese refugees in Uganda as in July 1996, when they massacred 115 of them in the Achol-Pii refugee camp.

Not much later 10th October 1996 they abducted more than 139 schoolgirls from St Mary's College in Aboke and took them to South

Sudan. About 20 of them managed to escape. The Belgian journalist Els de Temmerman wrote a book about the plight of the girls and the struggle of Sr Rachel to get them released and brought back to Uganda. She got support for her campaign even from the Pope and Kofi Annan, and she managed to get most of the girls back with the support of the presidents of Uganda, Sudan and South Africa.

This does not mean that the LRA has changed policy to recruit new soldiers by capturing children, especially among the Acholi, the Lango and Teso. They are often trained in Sudan to become young terrorists. It is said that since 1994 the LRA has abducted in this fashion more than 20,000 children, not even one third of them managing to escape. They are boys and girls between the age of 12 and 14. The LRA seems to see this age group as easiest to indoctrinate and to intimidate into killing others. The young girls are used as sex slaves and as wives for the officers. Worst of all, Kony is doing this to the Acholi, his own people. The young children are abducted at gunpoint, food and cattle looted, houses burned down. The children are forced to carry the loot. Those who refuse or try to run away are killed in front of the others.

This has been going on for years and I can understand Victor's fear. In 1997, Victor tells me, the situation was so bad that people in his village did not dare sleep at home anymore. In the evening they would move to the hospital and church compounds in town to sleep. Those were the few places guarded by the Ugandan army. But they were afraid that the LRA would attack the hospital to steal medicine as in the past. Victor, his parents and siblings slept there. But even during a war people have to live, cultivate their fields and go to school. During the day most people went home to their own neighbourhood. Victor has discovered that I am not only interested in the Sudanese, so he is quite willing to talk about his war experience.

While the Ugandan army was guarding the hospital, Victor was captured near home, coming from school with other children. Suddenly their captors were all around them with their weapons. Many of the soldiers were boys not much older than himself, and that is how he knew they were LRA and not ordinary robbers. They were young but they were not children anymore in their behaviour. They carried guns and machetes and they hacked to pieces the first child who tried to escape. Victor also wanted to run but he was paralysed. They made it clear that anybody who tried to escape would be hacked to pieces in the same way. It all happened near Victor's home and he thinks they killed his father before burning the house. Victor does not tell me how fearful he was, for when this happened to him he was about 13. He only tells me that together with twelve other boys and girls he was abducted and taken into the bush. He does not remember the exact route followed but he does remember the date: 11th February 1997.

They were on the road for quite a number of days, with hardly a chance to rest and very little to eat. They carried food stolen in Victor's village, plus food looted on the way. But they seemed to have forgotten water. "The worst was the thirst," Victor says, "A few boys died of it, others survived because they were ordered to drink each other's urine." They did not know where they were going, but Victor guessed it was to Sudan, where some of his relatives and other children had been taken before. They were exhausted when they finally arrived at a camp in the bush. He did not know it then, but he knows now that the camp was Joseph Kony's.

There he received his training and was taught how to use a gun. He did not want to be a soldier, but on seeing another boy who did not cooperate being hacked to pieces with an axe by other children, he thought it wiser to comply. Victor confirms all the terrible stories about the LRA I had heard from others.

It was cold in their training camp and the trainees got very little to eat in order to force them to go and steal food from the fields and to motivate them to join the trips to Uganda to rob and steal food. They not only learned how to use a gun; they were also taught how to use a machete. They really were trained to kill.

The life of the girls was not any easier; they often had it rougher than Victor. In many ways they were trained like boys, but on top of that they were forced to give sexual services to the older soldiers who often gang-raped them. Some of them felt lucky when soldiers chose them as wives, then at least they would be left alone by other soldiers. Victor saw a girl from his own village, not more than twelve, already pregnant. The girls were more carefully guarded than the boys. Kony considered them to be extra security for the LRA, because the Ugandan army are hesitant to attack a camp with many young girls. Kony uses them often as a human shield, threatening to kill the girls and the children if the camp is attacked.

Victor Onweng became a child-soldier in the army of the LRA. We don't talk about how free he was or whether he tried to escape. It is obvious that those who have to do the killing in this army are victims themselves. At times they were given drugs before they went on a mission in Uganda. Also they were anointed with oil to protect them against the bullets of the SPLA or the Ugandan army, but Victor saw many die from such bullets.

On one occasion Victor was taken on a mission to Uganda, not for the first time. When in his own village he covered his face so that people would not recognise him. It was all part of the military training, which usually takes four months. Victor had lost count of the days and weeks but he did not think that he had finished four months when he went on this mission to Uganda.

Then Victor tells me that he and three other boys decided to escape from the LRA. But when trying to escape from the LRA they ran into an ambush by the Ugandan army. There was an exchange of fire and the magic oil did not protect him. Victor shows me the scars. He and two others were caught by the Ugandan soldiers. They were astonished that they were not killed, as people who run into an ambush of the LRA are certainly killed. This they had been told during their training. The soldiers even bandaged his wounds and there was a lot of talk on their radio. An army helicopter landed next to them. It all was very scary as they did not know what was going to happen next. Victor and the others were flown to Lukung dispensary. After some days he could walk again.

He did not know where to turn to. If the LRA found him they would certainly kill him as a deserter. The people here would chase him away on finding out that he had been with Kony.

One of the soldiers, who saw how scared he was, took Victor to Gulu and brought him to a centre with more boys and girls who had escaped from the LRA. In the camp in Sudan they had been told about these places, adding that they would be bewitched if they went there. Victor had not gone there freely but he had been brought there.

He remembers a kind man called George Omona. He introduced Victor to other children, who told him that this was a good place. And it was good. There was food, medical care and counselling, to help them come to terms with the violence they had suffered and committed. Victor did not think the place was bad. But he found it hard to sleep because other children were screaming in their sleep. He also was afraid that the LRA would come and take him back to Sudan and kill him in front of the others as an example. People told him that he did not have to be afraid of the LRA as here there were soldiers of the Ugandan army to protect him. But the people who said these things had not been in the LRA and did not know that the soldiers of Kony were not afraid of the Ugandan army. At times he wanted to flee but he did not know where to flee to and he was afraid to go back to his own village. It was easy for people in the centre to tell him that what had happened was not his fault, but he was afraid that somebody had recognised him when he raided his village with the LRA. It took time, but gradually he settled again.

George Omona was the programme co-ordinator of Gulu Support the Children Organisation (GUSCO) since its beginning in 1995 until 2002. This Uganda charity works with children like Victor traumatised by war. They also work with teachers and other people who come into contact with these children, in order to help them to return to their communities. Victor is not the only one who is grateful for what George Omona is doing. In 2000 he received the Anti-Slavery award for his outstanding work with children abducted by the LRA. GUSCO, at that time, had rehabilitated more than 2,300 children.

Victor tells me that George helped him to go to school again. He talked to Alice, who Victor says is Dutch like me, and Alice is a friend of Sr Sophie. I try to figure out who this Alice might be. On asking Sr Sophie she smiled. Alice is Els (very often pronounced as Alice) de Temmerman. She has supported many escapees from the LRA by paying their school fees.

Victor wanted to go to school again but not in the part of Uganda where he was captured. Els talked to Sr Sophie about it. She hesitated. It was not easy to have ex-child-soldiers of the SPLA and the LRA in the same school, for at times they had fought each other in South Sudan. Sr Sophie, however, did not see this only as a problem but also as a challenge. Victor got a place in this school and he did not always find it easy but he feels that he gets an education that many of his own people do not, as they still live in daily fear of the LRA.

Victor has talked for hours. I have only asked a question now and again to prod him on. A few days ago he did not want to talk, but now he does not need much encouragement to do so. His voice and face change when relating the more terrible things, which he had to do or suffer. Now and again he falters as if not being quite sure what to tell and what to keep to himself.

After all this I would have expected Victor to be a much-traumatised child. He possibly is. He is a bit withdrawn, but gives the impression of being able to face life again. They are not treated here as traumatised or victims of war, but more as survivors with personal resources. Possibly that is the best way to help traumatised children in their healing process. Expertise in this field does not count for much.

Victor has been back to his village where he met his mother. His father was killed by the LRA. He did not want to stay there. Perhaps he will return after finishing secondary school. His home area is far from safe and the LRA try to recapture escapees. For the time being this school is not only school but also home.

Victor Onweng's story is the story of thousands of children who escaped from the LRA or were captured in battle against the army of Kony. A much greater number have not been able to return. It is estimated that since the LRA started abducting children in 1992/ 1993 more than 20,000 of them have been abducted, one third of them girls. From the beginning of the Operation Iron Fist (March 2002) to the end of 2003, according to UNICEF, a further 10,000 children have been abducted.

Victor and I talked for the first time some years ago. A few things have changed since. The world has become more aware of the atrocities committed by the LRA. After 11th September the Americans listed the LRA as a "terrorist" organisation. The GOS chose to join the anti-terrorist alliance rather than being named "terrorist" themselves. They could no longer openly support the LRA.

Under pressure from the West, the Government of Sudan has agreed not to support the Lord's Resistance Army any longer. In a few cases they have also assisted escapees from the LRA camps. Also Museveni, the president of Uganda, wants the children and youth to be returned to their homes. With permission of the GOS the Uganda army has gone into Sudan to drive the LRA back into Uganda. Unlike Victor, they probably underestimated the LRA, which fought back fiercely like cornered animals. Whole villages were burned down and hundreds of people killed by LRA soldiers, most of whom had been abducted from their homes as children.

In the Ugandan papers I read reports about the new attacks by the LRA, and new promises by the Ugandan government to defeat Kony's troops very soon now.

On my way from Entebbe to London I sit in the plane next to a Ugandan working in London. He sees me reading a book about Alice Lakwena and wonders at my interest. When I tell him about meeting victims of the LRA like Victor, we get talking. He calls himself an Acholi intellectual, one of the organisers of the *Kacoke Madit*, the big meeting of the Acholi. He tells me about how they consulted Acholi people all over the world. They produced big reports about bringing peace to Northern Uganda. They brought more than 150 delegates together, but neither Kony nor Museveni were there. They blamed the LRA, they blamed the Sudanese government; others blamed Museveni and the Ugandan army. Most of what was said was true: many different factors play a role in this war. The war in north of Uganda continues not only because the LRA is stronger or better equipped than the Ugandan army. There are politicians who want this war to continue, others have economic interests in this war.

My neighbour the Acholi intellectual tries to explain it all to me. Many peace initiatives have taken place since the conflict began. From 1986 elders like Mzee Tiberio Okeny were involved. The government took some initiative; my neighbour mentions Minister Betty Bigombe's in 1993-94. In 2000 there was an amnesty. Peace teams were set up in the Acholi districts, a presidential peace team was set up and various attempts were made by traditional leaders in collaboration with the religious leaders of the interfaith group of the north of Uganda and the south of Sudan. He asks whether I have ever heard of Archbishop Odama of Gulu and Bishop Paride Taban from Sudan. When I tell him that I work closely with Bishop Taban and that I have met Archbishop Odama once, he shakes my hand and tells me that his name is Caesar. He knows both bishops and he has listened to them at the meeting of the religious leaders. He tells me how Archbishop Odama and other religious leaders slept in the streets of Gulu together with thousands of people from around the area, who come into town in the evening to be safe from LRA attacks and abductions. He suggests that I must try to meet these church leaders.

Caesar knows the latest figures: 1.2 million people have been displaced in the north of Uganda, especially Acholi, Teso and Lango.

This war has been going on for more than 17 years now and most children haven't had much of a chance to go to school. With regard to that, Victor was perhaps lucky to have been abducted; without it he would probably never have had the opportunity to go to Blessed Damian. In this war women and children seem to be the main victims, many of them staying in camps for the displaced, without being able to go home soon. They are not only victims of the LRA but also often targets of other armed groups. Uprooted from their home and cultural values these people get traumatised, some commit suicide. Besides the guns many are victims of the other killers, HIV and AIDS.

We talk about hope for peace. I tell him about Bishop Taban's efforts and people on the other side of the border. We have common friends, and in Africa it is said, "The friends of my friends are my friends."

My friend tells me how they have appealed to the UN for assistance in what he calls "one of the world's worst crises." Humanitarian assistance is not enough. He doesn't believe in a military solution, despite promises by the Ugandan government to destroy the LRA within weeks. Caesar is inclined to agree with Archbishop Odama that peaceful dialogue is the only way to bring an end to the war. The people are tired of it, but at times one gets the impression that the two armies, the government's and Kony's, want the war to continue. We are still without solution when landing at Heathrow. We travelled together in 2003 and occasionally we hear from each other.

The beginning of 2004 is not better than 2003. This becomes clear to me during a visit to Gulu. I am the guest of Catholic Archbishop of Gulu, Archbishop Odama, two days after about 200 IDPs have been butchered by the LRA in Barlonyo camp near Lira, in February 2004. It is not only a tremendous shock, it is also a big embarrassment to the government who claimed a few days ago that they had the LRA nearly under control. During a demonstration in Lira, pleading for security, riots broke out and 5 Acholi were killed by the local people of Lira, the Langi.

Archbishop Odama, and the retired bishop of Kitgum of the Anglican Church sit together on the veranda of the bishop's house in Gulu. They are busy with a peace and reconciliation apostolate via their mobile phones, talking to the church leaders in Lira, talking to newspapers, sending messages to the radio in Lira in the hope that they can prevent that the riots turn into ethnic clashes between the Langi and the Acholi. Some people have started to equate the Acholi with the LRA, but the bishops explain in their radio message that the Acholi and the Langi both are abducted by the LRA. The religious leaders are worried that the local militias will start fighting other local militias and that the people in Northern Uganda will start killing each other as has happened in Southern Sudan. The government talks about more troops to defeat the LRA, these bishops talk about dialogue and reconciliation.

By now 920,000 people have been displaced for more than 7 years. Thousands of children walk every evening from the surroundings of Gulu into the dusty town, to sleep on the sidewalks of the streets. In town there is protection from the army, at home they don't feel safe at night any longer. The Interfaith group of religious leaders feel concerned, they represent the Orthodox Church, the Muslims, the Anglican Church and the Catholic Church. The fact that also they cannot solve this war does not mean they do nothing, they try to stress the sacredness of life. They keep stressing that protection of children is not just accomplished by the gun, but especially by love. They at least try to make the world aware of what is happening here. They joined the thousands of children and slept with them in the streets to show their solidarity.

They didn't sleep all that much, the bishops tell me, but they talked a lot. They tried to listen to the children who came with more questions then they could answer. Archbishop Odama explains to me that even when you can't answer questions you can pass them on to the people concerned. Bishop Ochola remembers the questions clearly. When he talks about them it is clear that these are not only the questions of children but that they are also his own questions.

The children would like to ask the LRA: "Why do you target us children for abduction to fight in a war which we don't understand." The religious leaders have tried to start a few times a dialogue with the LRA, but they were disrupted by the military. Many wonder whether the military wants the war to continue.

The children are asking the government: "You are supposed to protect us, why are you not doing it, many of us are abducted from our homes, from the schools, even from the camps which you started for our security. Where is your protection?" The government is claiming that it does all it can, but it only seems to believe in a military solution. The religious leaders know that without reconciliation there will be no permanent solution.

The children are asking the world: "Why do you not raise our voices?" The religious leaders are passing on these questions. The two bishops are just back from a journey to the USA and Europe, lobbying for understanding and support.

Archbishop Odama says that the LRA has not answered the question of the children. Also the government has no clear answers. The world community is slowly starting to respond and shows willingness to help. But with a tired look he adds; "It is too slow."

As we are talking the Archbishop gets a phone call that trouble is brewing in town, a kiosk of a Langi trader has been set on fire after somebody shouted that in Lira the Langi are killing the Acholi. The Archbishop and the Bishop don't hesitate a minute but they jump in the car and drive into Gulu, encouraging the people to remain calm. Also the army and police are keeping an eye on the situation and after an hour they return, glad that the situation is calm again.

I have just read that President Museveni has said that dialogue has failed, Archbishop Odama smiles with a tired look on his face as he explains that we can never give up the dialogue. He points out that the dialogue fits better in with the African culture. But even in a Western rational approach it must be obvious that dialogue is cheaper; you don't need expensive weapons, no costly infrastructure, it doesn't cost many lives like the armed struggle. But what is even more important to him is that you can have a dialogue without having winners or losers, that in the end it is all about reconciliation and restoring relations.

Bishop Ochola points out that the military approach has not been successful either and that the dialogue hasn't really been tried. Archbishop Odama is a strong believer in the dialogue and he points out that it still has a chance after all that has happened. He says: "Africans often have a short memory of hatred. They are not looking for retributive justice, but for restorative justice. For us Africans restoration of relations is more important than retributive justice. We are willing to forget what has happened if we can restore the relations. The one who has committed the crime is brought back to the community where he or she belongs. We need reconciliation in so many fields. Even if the LRA is defeated militarily that does not mean that there will be peace. So much injustice has happened that the victims never can be compensated, but through dialogue which might take a long time relations can be restored."

It is Ash Wednesday 2004 when we sit together in the dark on the veranda of the bishop's house in Gulu and admire these bishops who haven't given up hope and who keep fighting in their own way for true peace in Uganda.

I think of Victor and our talk in Blessed Damian, I have lost touch with him but I hope that he soon can go home and enjoy this peace and help to build up his country.

"Lucky" Jacinta

"A child who turns out good is often not reared on a beautiful mat."

(Akan proverb)

Jacinta's luck was that she, a girl, did actually finish primary school. After the 1972 Addis Ababa agreement the missionaries returned to South Sudan, continuing the work they did before their expulsion in 1964. The Comboni Sisters saw the importance of education for girls, for whom they opened a school in Nzara. Not everybody was convinced that girls should be sent to school. But Jacinta's mother and her uncles encouraged and supported her. It had not been easy to find a good school near the place where her mother worked. Luckily the Nzara sisters provided boarding facilities to which Jacinta was admitted. She finished primary school in a refugee camp in the Central African Republic, where she fled with her uncles and with government troops on the run from Yambio and Nzara ahead of the advancing SPLA in 1990. Her mother had fled in the opposite direction when the SPLA liberated Maridi, some time after her daughter had fled from Nzara. She ended up in a refugee camp in Zaïre, present day Congo. In 1990 many people in Western Equatoria fled the Sudan war to neighbouring countries: Congo, the Central African Republic or Uganda. The priests, Sisters and some missionaries fled with the people and lived with them in the refugee camps.

The Comboni Sisters fled on the 21st November 1991 to the Central African Republic. Jacinta and other girls followed them and that is how she was able to finish her primary education.

A few months earlier I myself had been encouraged to flee via Congo and Kenya to the Netherlands. We expatriates always seem to get a chance to get away when things become really dangerous. I went home, whereas the people I was working with had to flee from their homes to neighbouring countries. It was a wise decision but it still gave me the feeling of a deserter.

Jacinta's mother was a nurse in a refugee camp in Zaire. Often she thought of home, the fertile Azande land with more mangoes than people could eat. She thought a lot of her daughter, a refugee in another country. The family, as was often the case, was scattered all over the Congo, the Central African Republic and Uganda. Those with nothing to lose were still in Sudan, hiding in the forests of Western Equatoria.

When Jacinta's mother heard that the Comboni Sisters had returned to Nzara in May 1991, she decided to return to Sudan from the Congo. I was returning to the area at the same time. The missionaries' return to the area liberated a year earlier by the SPLA meant for many that it must be fairly safe to go home. She had also heard that the Comboni Sisters had started a leper and TB hospital. She hoped to be able to work there. In the past she had worked in a government hospital, but she knew the Comboni Sisters from her visits to her daughter in Nzara. She got a job and some living quarters near the hospital.

Jacinta meanwhile had been staying with her uncles in Mboki, a refugee camp in the Central African Republic. Her father had died years earlier. Her uncles played father to her and she stayed with them till she finished primary school. After finishing primary school she felt lucky to be able to go home and stay with her mother in Nzara. The mother was glad to see her daughter again. She had called her Minallah (a gift from God) at birth. Later on she had been baptised Jacinta. She lived with her mother and her friends Veronica and Miriam near the hospital. They were glad to be back in Sudan. But the soldiers of the SPLA were also happy to see these young ladies, about 16 years old. They did not make life easy for them. Often they demanded more than the girls were willing to give. The mother found it a heavy responsibility to bring up her daughter by herself. She also felt responsible for the girl's friends who lived with her.

She went to see Sr Natalia, the superior of the Nzara community. Her small stature is more than compensated by her exceptional courage. She was certainly not intimidated by the big Dinka SPLA soldiers. When she gave them a piece of her mind they did not dare to look down upon her, they just looked away. She stood up for the girls. It did not always make her popular with the SPLA, but then, for Sr Natalia, being a missionary is not about being popular. But she did not want a quarrel with the soldiers all the time and the two women sought a better solution. They dreamed about secondary education for the girls.

While searching, Sr Natalia gave the girls a hut on the compound of the sisters' convent. There was hardly any secondary education for girls in Southern Sudan. I used to visit the Sisters every now and then. Jacinta and other girls were learning embroidery. On many evenings Sr Natalia talked to them after work. The darkness, as darkness often does, seemed to invite them to be more truthful. By sharing their lives they became true friends. There I met Jacinta more than ten years ago, but I lost track of her on being no longer stationed in Western Equatoria, and Sr Natalia having moved to Uganda. Before leaving she managed to find a place for Jacinta in Aboke Girls' Secondary in Uganda with the Comboni missionaries, who took pity on her to the point of flying Jacinta and her friends in a small aircraft to Uganda. Jacinta was no longer a refugee at that time; she was a lucky Sudanese girl studying abroad.

A few days ago Sr Natalia and I met in Kampala, and reminisced about Southern Sudan. We shared a lot of memories, good and bad. Many people we knew had died, others had gone abroad and others yet had returned from Congo and from the Central African Republic.

Did I remember Jacinta?, Sr Natalia wondered. Of course I did. I was told that Jacinta also remembered me. She had been briefly in Kampala from the Kiriadongo refugee camp. I asked for news. Sr Natalia said, "I am proud of her, but Jacinta is still going through hard times." She was silent for a moment as if considering what to say. Then she pulled a letter out of her pocked and said, "I don't think I'm betraying any trust." The letter had been written a few weeks earlier. It was in a very neat handwriting and very good English. I read it to myself. After the usual introductory greetings and wishes for Sr Natalia, the letter went on:

"My aim in writing to you is that my mind and heart are very heavy and I feel that I should share them with you. It is now 11:50 p.m. and I can't sleep. That is why I am writing. I am so very tired. It looks as if I am fighting a losing battle. I feel both exhausted and frustrated. I have come to realise now that I am very unlucky and my life seems full only of misfortunes.

To begin with, last week I went for interviews at the Interaid office in old Kampala. They wanted to sponsor refugees for computer training. I passed the interview together with some other refugees. We were told to come today to pick our admission letters. But today they were sorry to inform me that the funds were not enough and I had to wait for another chance next year, when the present group complete their course. I could hardly believe my ears. I nearly fainted on realising I was the only one not admitted among the selected. I have come to hate myself to the extent of being sorry to have been born. At moments like this I only wish to die. I am too tired to tackle the problems that come my way.

I don't know which office I have not been to, seeking a chance to go back to school for further education. I have tried everywhere, I have tried my best and all in vain. Some who claim that they want to help me to go back to school want the use of my body in return. I don't want this kind of help and in the end I lose another chance. At other places they consider tribal

92

affiliation, and there is no one of my tribe who can help me. I went to the Church of Uganda as they had scholarships and also to Across, but they were sponsoring Madi or Acholi students only, not others. In the refugee camp I was supposed to be teaching English but the Acholis refused to give me the job because I was not an Acholi. Also, some teachers in the school with whom I was teaching in 2000 wanted me, but I refused. We all started hating each other. As at the moment of writing they face the problem of not having an English teacher. Yet they refuse to give me the job, picking instead an Acholi qualified in religion and political science to teach English.

I don't know how long I will be able to live in this situation. My friends look down on me as a failure in life, yet they know I did not fail my exams. They think I am a liar, as all I said and hoped for does not seem to happen the way it should. I am now almost three years without a job.

I have tried a lot, even raising poultry in the camp. I borrowed the money and went to my aunt in Entebbe as she works there with people who hatch chicks. To my surprise she told me that their machine had broken down. She suggested leaving the money with her for her to ring me when the chicks started hatching again for me to collect them. The chicks hatched but she kept them. When I try to see her she hides. What to do, she is my aunt and I have decided to forget about it.

Although the Bible says that 'God's ways are not our ways and that God's thoughts are not our thoughts' I have become confused through all that is happening to me. Nothing seems to work out; I have tried for jobs everywhere. I have tried to work as a house girl but to no avail. I got one job with Care International, they wanted me to go to New Sudan and I accepted. I wanted to go home and this was a chance. Then all of a sudden they told me to wait for their call. From the beginning of the year I have been waiting for their call and I am still waiting but not a word from them. I was offered another job as a volunteer worker, again in New Sudan, they too promised to call me when it is time to go. Up to now there has been not a word.

I started to work for the Joint Voluntary Agency and the US Refugee Programme here in Kampala when they came to conduct interviews for taking refugees for settlement in America. The J.V.A.'s field team leader said my file with them was very good; therefore they wanted to employ me as a permanent worker and not just as a volunteer. But the people here in Uganda refused to take me on for reasons best known to themselves. What haven't I tried?

I have done embroidery work, which you encouraged me to do, till I developed eye problems. As I am writing I fail to see what I still can do or how I can improve my life. Fr John in the camp tried to find someone to pay my fees but all in vain and in the end even he had to give up.

Now my people are telling me that all these misfortunes are happening to me because I failed to provide all those uncles and aunties with what they demanded of me. That is the reason why I can't succeed, they say. I am confused now and I don't know what is what anymore. I had decided that I would pay them on getting a job but I have failed to get one. I have changed my mind. In case I finish the four sets of tablecloths I am working on currently, I can go to them. There is nothing much I can do at the moment.

Here in Kampala I had got one NGO to pay for me but on condition that I join their Church, called Greater Grace in Mengo, Kampala. They made a lot of promises but when I refused to join their Church they refused to help me. Anyway I just told them that I can't change my Church for any worldly gains. Now they are annoyed with me and they have stopped coming to my home.

Anyway, if I am going on writing it will be too much for you, so let me stop. I thank you very much for sharing your time with me by reading this disturbing letter. Thank you very much for your kindness and love towards all of us. I appreciate all you have done for us. I only pray that God will continue to bless you and give you strength and good health so that you go on with your daily task.

Please don't worry over what I have written. I just want to share my feelings with you. This month I am very close to my parents since it is a month dedicated to them in a special way. I keep on believing that by next year something will come out of all of this if God allows it. Not my will but His be done.

May God bless you and keep you safe, thanks, Yours sincerely, Minallah Jacinta."

What a letter, what a life, I don't know what to say, and I look at Sr Natalia. She tells me she has talked to Jacinta and told her that I am in town. Jacinta wants to meet me again. She wants to leave it to Jacinta what she wants to tell about her life and what she wants to hold back since our meeting in Nzara. Sr Natalia has been in touch with her all these years. She reaches Jacinta at her Kampala phone number. Jacinta promises to come to visit me. I tell her that I am looking forward to seeing her again.

This afternoon we meet in the garden of the Mill Hill Guest-house in Kampala. I hardly recognised Jacinta in this well but simply dressed woman. We talk first about Sr Natalia. Jacinta says how lucky she had felt when Sr Natalia found her a place in St Mary's Secondary School of Aboke in the north of Uganda. It was 1993. The first few years everything went very well for her. But her mother felt it safer to flee from Sudan to Uganda in 1994 when it seemed likely that the government was going to attack Nzara again. Fleeing from home a second time within a few years had been hard for her mother. But Jacinta felt lucky. Her mother was in Kiriadongo refugee camp, not far.

Jacinta was going to be a well educated African girl, she was going to make it. She was intelligent and willing to work hard to pass her exams, so as not to shame her mother and uncles who had supported her. Also Sr Natalia should be proud of her. All went well till that 9th October night in 1996.

That night stands out in her life; together with 130 other girls she was abducted by the LRA rebels. I had read about this abduction in the book by Els de Temmerman,[2] but not for one moment had I thought I actually knew one of the girls. Strange how a story changes when somebody one knows is in it. I don't tell Jacinta about having read of her ordeal, I let her tell her story. She has no difficulty talking about it, as I am not the first person she relates her nightmare to. Sr Natalia also knew, but perhaps it was better to leave it to Jacinta to talk about that unlucky night and following days.

She says:

"We were woken up by people banging on the door of our dormitory. Men shouted for us to open the doors. We were afraid. We tried to hide under the beds and some girls started crying in fear. When we did not open the door they started breaking the windows. Some jumped in, shining torches on our faces, and then opened the doors. Some 100 men surrounded us. They tied us together with ropes in groups of four or five and brought us outside. We were very afraid. We knew they were LRA men, about whom we had heard the most horrible stories. Many of them were boys, who seemed to know some of the girls. Later we realised that they were boys of the Samuel Baker School in Gulu, who had been abducted earlier. We had been told how cruel they could be, and trembled even thinking about them. They marched us to the gate and told us that we would survive if we obeyed their orders. The rules were simple: "Don't talk during the journey; if you do we padlock your mouth or cut off your lips. If you cry we pluck out your eyes." They were not joking.

We were marched behind the church. As we came to the bush they started picking out young girls under eleven and told them to go back. In the process they raped a young girl from Gulu, perhaps as a warning of what would happen if we did not obey. On arriving at the next village they went to the house of a certain woman and shouted for her to open the door. She refused. They kicked the door open and dragged her out struggling. They held her and said: "Who do you think you are, struggling with us. We'll teach you a lesson." They started beating her with sticks, telling us

---

[2] *Aboke Girls, Children Abducted in Northern Uganda* by Els de Temmerman, Fountain publisher, ISBN 9970 02 256 3.

to watch so as to learn what happens to those who don't cooperate with them. A half-drunken man, back from the Independence Day dance, staggered into this and started shouting. Some of the soldiers started shooting and in the turmoil I dived into the bush. As I tried to crawl away they flashed a torch in my face and shot in the air. I was very afraid. They marched me back to the group and now they really tied us up very well. We walked through the night. One young soldier came to Caroline Onyango, the girl before me. She is still with them today. He told her not to worry, as he had already chosen her to be his wife on coming to the camp. It only made me worry more. During the night I tried again to escape but in vain.

As morning approached we had no more chances to escape. As light broke we arrived at a swamp. They told us that on the other side of the swamp they had prepared a place for us with food and dry clothes. It was difficult to cross the swamp tied as we were, and the water up to our necks. One girl fell and we had to pull her up again. But at the end we saw a bit of a hill on the other side.

When we reached the small hill on the other side young rebels were cutting sticks meant to cane us with. They divided us and we had to sit down waiting for the order to be caned, but one of the rebels in charge was still talking on the radio with Kony. He was told that the Ugandan army now knew that we were abducted and they were looking for us. All of a sudden we heard a plane and they thought it was the helicopter of the UPDF. The rebels chased us quickly into the bush to hide us. We fell over each other as the aircraft flew over, after which we were brought back

It was about eleven when they told us that a Sister had been following us. "What is wrong with that *muzungu*[3] to interfere with our affairs. We will teach her a lesson," one of them said. They surrounded Sr Rachele and our teacher John Bosco who had followed us. They took a very threatening attitude but Sr Rachele was unperturbed. They said to her: "Why have you come, do you

---

[3] *Muzungu* means white person. It is a term going back to colonial days and often it expresses some contempt for white people.

see any white people here, we are only taking our own children to where they belong." Sr Rachele answered that the parents had entrusted us to her care, that she had the right to follow us and that she could not go back without us.

They said that if she did not go back they would break our right arms. She told them to break her arm first. Then they said they would cut off our lips. Sr Rachele told them that she could not allow this and that they should cut off hers first. The rebels did not know what to do with this Sister and said, "Are you ready to move with us?" Sister answered: "I will go where the girls go."

And she did come with us. We marched on with Sr Rachele encouraging us not to give up hope, saying that with God everything is possible. On seeing that a girl nearly collapsed under the load she had to carry, Sister talked to the rebels and they told others to take the load. She also kept pleading with them to let her go back with the girls. They only answered: "Let us go ahead, we shall release them but let them first carry our luggage to a certain place." Sister told us that she thought that they might release us, but she wasn't sure.

About 2 p.m. they heard on the radio that the army helicopter had left Gulu to search for us. We were told to get branches to camouflage us so as not to be seen. But the helicopter flew very low and the rebels told Sr Rachele to take off her white veil so that she would not be seen from the air. She did so and put it in her pocket. Even the rebels themselves were afraid now. One of the commanders, the one with a swollen lip was praying, and told the sister to pray too for us not to be seen. We hid in a banana plantation and when the helicopter left we were rushed on to another place. Sr Rachele kept pleading for them to let us go, as it was already getting late.

We came to an open place, where we were welcomed by an old man: "My dear daughters, I have waited for you many years, I have planted these bananas for you and this is your home." There was a young boy walking around who had been shot in the buttocks. The Sister walked up to him and started treating him. The rebels offered her a cup of tea, as *wazungu*[4] are

---

[4] *Wazungu* is the kiswahili name for the white people.

always very weak, they said. She asked that we should also be given tea, but they refused, as they said the looted sugar would not be enough. We were left with some rebels guarding us. Others went for a meeting. We waited and waited.

When they came back, some sat around and started sharpening their knives in a very threatening way. We became afraid again and we held our breath. It looked as if they were going to butcher us and that we were facing our last hour.

They looked at a girl from Soroti, who was very fat and had difficulty walking with her bruised legs. "She is useless," they said, and told her to go and sit on the other side. Then they looked at me. One of them said that he thought that I had tried to escape. They told me to sit with the fat girl. I was afraid, as they were lighting a fire and we had heard that they cook people. They were still threatening us with the *pangas*.[5] I was sweating but I also felt cold. They started asking the girls their names, the names of their parents and chiefs. They knew many of them. They praised some but disparaged others. They divided us into two groups, according to their liking or disliking our parents or relatives. Our group became very big, in the end we were more than a hundred, the other group was small, maybe thirty. They told Sister that she could go back with the big group but they would take the small group with them. But Sr Rachele pleaded to let all the girls go back, now that they had carried the luggage this far. They became angry and said that if she did not do what she was told they would take the lot. We did not know what to do. The girls of the small group pleaded with Sister for her to go back with the big group, in which they spotted some of their own sisters.

The Sister agreed in the end. She gave a piece of paper to the girls in the small group for them to write something to their parents, but most were so upset that they could not even construct one sentence. Some started pleading with the sister; "Don't leave us, as tonight we will be raped." Sister doubted again and the rebels, very angry by now, started beating the girls. Other girls in the small group pleaded with us to go, otherwise the rebels would get angrier.

---

[5]   A *panga* is a multi-use African machete for cutting small trees as well as for butchering.

The sister accepted and we walked away. We walked all the evening through the night till morning, when we reached Otwal railway station. Here we sent a message to the school that we were coming, and Sr Alba came to collect us together with some of the parents. We were lucky that we survived, maybe thanks to the Sister."

Jacinta stops here to drink some water. She looks tired now, as telling me this story is like reliving it. I knew, from having read about the journey of the small group, that Jacinta was really lucky to have been in the group allowed to go back with Sr Rachele. I had met Sr Rachele in Holland for the launching of Els de Temmerman's "The Aboke girls," in which she tells the story of the unlucky ones who went with the rebels into the Sudan. Sr Rachele struck me as a brave little woman who cared for her girls. I look now at Jacinta and I realise how brave she also is, especially when after a brief pause, without my pushing for more, she is willing to go on with the story of her life.

She did not dare to stay in Aboke, as the rebels had promised to come back. She decided to go back to her mother in the refugee camp, together with another girl with whom she had been abducted. They had been the lucky ones, they had got away and they did not want to take any more chances. They wanted to get away from Gulu. Life in a refugee camp was better than living in constant fear of the LRA. But near Karuma bridge the bus they were travelling in ran into an LRA ambush, another ordeal with guns against her head. This time she doesn't go into details. She shakes her head and says: "Ah, it was really terrible." Jacinta escaped once more without being harmed physically. She was the lucky one; her friend was not, for she lost a leg in the ambush.

At home with her mother she went through a difficult time. She wanted to go back to school but it was as if she could not learn anymore. In her sleep the rebels pointed guns at her head and they were still sharpening their knives. She went back to Masindi High School, sponsored by the diocese of Torit. But she could not study and she was often sick.

She struggled on, convinced that only with education would she be able to face the future. She finished her secondary school and went to Mbarara where she started senior secondary. Ever so often her studies were interrupted because her mother became sick and she went to look after her. Her brother became a criminal. He tried to rob JRS, but landed in prison. Jacinta in no way approved of her brother but he was her brother and she struggled and paid the fine to get him out. The consequence was that she had no money to pay the school fees. When she finally found another sponsor she heard that her mother had had a stroke. She saw it as her duty to find a doctor for her mother in Kampala. She had it all arranged when she sat for her final examinations. After the examinations she would take her mother to hospital. The examinations were on the 8th December 1999. Jacinta does not mention dates very often, but the way she mentions the 8th December 1999, I have the impression that it is another date like when she was abducted. She rushed home the day after the examinations to take her mother to hospital.

But when she arrived "home" in the refugee camp she only found a grave. Her mother had been buried the previous day. Nobody had informed Jacinta; perhaps they did not know where to reach her. Maternal uncles had paid for the funeral as their traditions require, but expected her to pay them back.

Something broke in her, after all the years of struggling against all the difficulties. She wondered whether God really cared for her. She did not want anything to do with God; she did not pray anymore. She considered committing suicide. She was not afraid of death and she wanted to die. Jacinta tells me: "The only reason why I did not commit suicide was that if I killed myself I was afraid that I would not see my parents in the after life." Fr Tom in the refugee camp looked after her and listened to her. He sent her to a retreat centre in Jinja where she started to recover and get new strength. "I started to see again that suffering is part of our life," she says.

She went back to the camp where she began to teach English in the school. But suffering remained part of her life. Her criminal brother came with a gang and stole everything from her house. In spite of it all she struggled on.

She came to know all the organisations, NGOS and education sponsorship programmes for refugees in Uganda. She was not impressed. She was promised a sponsorship to study law in Dar es Salaam in the year 2000. When she arrived there she was told that she had to wait till 2001. In 2001 the money was finished. A relative of hers in the SPLA thought he could get her a sponsorship to study political science in Nairobi but for that she had to become a member of the SPLA. She was prepared to do that and go for the training. In the end she declined when she heard that most of the girls, who went through it before her, came back pregnant against their will. She told the commander that she would not go, if sleeping with the soldiers was one of the conditions. They had looked at her and said: "What is wrong with this girl, what is wrong with getting pregnant?" Their attitude hurt Jacinta. She would like to have children, but she also wants a father for them. She misses her own father who died when she still needed him. She had a boyfriend once, but when she discovered that he had another relationship with a friend of hers she broke with him.

The SPLA sponsorship would have allowed her to go back to South Sudan, which she sees as her real home. Now she considered going home once more, as the life of a refugee is not an easy one. Refugees are never really welcome, and who wants to die a slow death in a foreign country? Moreover Jacinta never fled from Sudan. She came to Uganda to get education because there were no educational opportunities in Sudan. But the opportunities for jobs in Sudan are few as long as the war continues. Jacinta has to earn some money to pay off her debts to her uncles. Two cousins live with her and she feels responsible for them. She came to the conclusion that she cannot afford to go home yet. There is support for the refugees, but very little for the internally displaced or for those who return home. She decided that for the time being she has to struggle on as refugee in Uganda.

For some time she was on a list of refugees bound for the US to study there. But the lists were constantly rearranged and in the end her name was erased from the list. She worked for a relief organisation and went with them to Sudan; she saw how food was diverted and how it was even taken back to Uganda. She had protested. Again her bosses had reacted as if there was something wrong with her. She did not give up and she applied for other jobs. She knows that she is intelligent, but she also knew that she would not get the job when the person who interviewed her in his private office only wanted to know whether she had a husband or whether she was still free and suggested that they meet later in a hotel. Her answer remained "no," even after some of her friends agreed to pay for their sponsorship or job with sexual favours.

Could I understand now why at times she was so desperate as to write to Sr Natalia the letter that she had shared with me?, she wonders. I think I understand. In a way I am astonished that she is not more desperate. I also realise that each issue she has talked about has hurt her very deeply and it is clear that such things have not happened only to Jacinta, but to many other women and girls from Sudan.

For the time being Jacinta is back in the refugee camp, living on her relief ration, making a bit of money with her embroidered table cloths and bed sheets which she sells in Kampala. In that way she is at least not dependent on anybody's demanding favours in return for whatever help they give. She has not given up struggling, fighting for a life where she and other women will be respected. But one cannot be in the forefront all the time; now and again one has to stop and think what to do next. But she still has to make a living for herself and those who depend on her.

She finds it a pity that her project with the chickens, which her aunt was going to get for her, went haywire. It would have been a good money spinner, for there is a market in the camp for eggs and for broilers. We talk about it. One chick in the government hatchery in Entebbe costs nearly half a dollar. Jacinta does not ask for money. I am just back from Europe and still have a few dollars from some friends. Jacinta thinks that fifty dollars would start her off with the poultry. I give her the fifty dollars.

After that I find it difficult to ask her to be allowed to share with others what she has told me, or to write down her story. I feel I have no right to publish her story without her permission. If I ask her now, she might think of it as a favour in return for the fifty dollars. It might confirm her opinion that every favour has a price. But this time I am the lucky one. She has heard from Sr Natalia that I have written a book about the plight of the people in South Sudan. She thinks that the world should also know about the plight of the Sudanese refugees, people like herself who have been blown away from Sudan all over the world.

Bishop Paride Taban
(photo by Mathew Haumann)

Fr Mathew Haumann (left) and Bishop Paride Taban

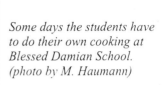

Opposite page:

*Nuba Mountains
(photo by Ferdinand von
Habsburg-Lothringen)*

*Some days the students have
to do their own cooking at
Blessed Damian School.
(photo by M. Haumann)*

*Sister Sophie Asiimwe
with one of the pupils
at Blessed Damian School.
(photo by
Mathew Haumann)*

Child soldier in the north of Uganda.
(Photo by Reanne Den Bodaert)

Yousif Kuwa Mekki (photo by Ferdinand von Habsburg-Lothringen)

Archbishop Odama of Gulu (Uganda)
and Bishop Paride Taban of Torit (Sudan).
(Three supporters of dialogue).

Rt Rev. Baker Ochola II
Retired Anglican Bishop of Kitgum

Gabriel Cardinal Zubeir Wako of Khartoum
(photo by Mathew Haumann)

Gabriel Cardinal Zubeir Wako with the displaced.

Camp for IDPs in Uganda

*Ex-child soldiers in
a school in Uganda
point out where home is.
(photo by Mathew Haumann)*

Sister Paskwina
(photo by Mathew Haumann)

Mrs Rebecca N. de Mabior
(photo by Mathew Haumann)

The Fourth Town

"Poverty makes you eat your fists."

(Ugandan proverb)

It is late in the evening when the plane lands in Khartoum. During the day the tarmac nearly melts under the heat of summer months, which at times reaches 48°C. Even now that it has become a little cooler, walking out of the plane is like walking into a sauna with your clothes on.

The airport has been done up and the reception is friendly enough, friendlier than I was used to in the late 1980s and early 1990s. I expected security to be very strict, as is the case in most of the world after 11th September. I can practically walk to the exit without having to open anything or being stopped by anybody. Maybe it is due to the fact that I am being collected by Mr Aladin, who brought my visa arranged by the Acropole Hotel where I spent my first nights. Aladin knows a few words of English and I even fewer words of Arabic, but he does not need words to express himself. We understand each other perfectly. Aladin drives me through the night and through the few checkpoints along the road, but he just smiles and waves and we are let through. Having worked for many years in South Sudan I have certainly been affected by the prejudices of the people in the South against the Arabs, that they cannot be trusted and that they despise other races. But I meet only friendliness.

The hotel is a wonderful mixture of the traditional and modern. In the dining hall one is served by servants dressed as they were in Khartoum 100 years ago. They know some English, but they do not need words as they know what you need before you do yourself. They are over-friendly, nearly subservient, an attitude not so often met with in South Sudan. The walls have pictures of what can be called tourist attractions in and around Khartoum: camel riding, ruins of the old kingdoms and traditional Dervish dances. But the biggest picture in the room is the painting, in a gilded frame, of the Sacred Heart of Jesus. The owners are Greek Orthodox and proud of it. In Sudan religion is seldom a private affair. It forms part of your identity, whether Muslim or Christian.

In the reception area one finds all the latest amenities for travellers including a cyber café. Most rooms have air-conditioning. Many of the guests seem to be from aid organizations and everybody seems to know everybody else. Quite a few are in the "helping industry." They know that many people in and around Khartoum would welcome their help but they are not so sure whether the government does too. At times the government seems to say yes and no at the same time by taxing their help very heavily.

Early in the morning I go into Khartoum with a friend who has worked with the displaced for years. It is hot, but there is no sun: there blows a strong hot wind and fine dust is everywhere. My driver calls the sandstorm *haboob*. The town has been greatly renovated of late; not all the oil money has been spent on the war, as is often claimed in the South. Quite a bit of it has been spent right here in Khartoum, on roads and new office buildings. I like the style and architecture of the new buildings going up; it is beautiful and colourful.

However, in spite of the better roads, new buildings and a new bridge across the Nile, the government has not been able to eliminate the traffic jams in the centres of Khartoum and Omdurman. They are hardly to be blamed; very few towns in Africa have solved that problem. From one of the bridges across the Nile I see the place where the White and Blue Nile merge. It is an impressive view even in the mist of fine sand. We have just passed Gordon's renovated palace close to the Nile. I have been reading about it in "The White Nile" by Alan Moorehead. I suppose that not only the Nile has not changed since Gordon lived here more than a century ago; Khartoum is a mixture of the old and the new. Sitting in a car with my Sudanese friend in a traffic jam I watch the people. Khartoum looks like a melting pot of ethnic and culturally very different people of Sudan. I understand why in colonial days Khartoum was a town of foreigners like Egyptians, Syrians, Greeks, Copts, Armenian, Turks and some British. As was the case those days there are many Arabs around, but I don't think they can be dubbed foreigners. Omdurman is the more African town, although in the time of the Mahdi it was more the government centre than Khartoum.

With a population of more than five million Khartoum has become one of the biggest capitals of Africa. I have read that it really consists of three towns; Khartoum, Omdurman and Khartoum North. Today it is obvious, especially in day time, that many people around us are from the South. Many dark southerners have fled the war in the South trying to find refuge or possibly work in Khartoum. They don't always feel welcome, and towards evening many have to leave the centre of town.

My friend tells me that most people here, like himself, have African rather than Arabic roots, and of course many are of mixed descent. He doesn't quite agree with the version that the capital consists of three towns; he wants to show me a fourth one. He knows that I have heard about displaced people in Khartoum, but he does not want to tell me more than I might have heard. He wants to show me where they live; for him seeing is believing.

The last time I saw this part of town was in 1990. It strikes me that many of the dirty slums where people used to live at that time under plastic and cardboard and in building sites on the outskirts of Omdurman have disappeared. On telling my friend about the perceived progress, he smiles and says: "Progress for whom?" We are crossing the spacious new bridge and he comments on how spacious it is, how well it is finished with concrete sideways and streetlights that work. I don't see anything special; to me the bridge looks what a bridge should look like. Across the bridge we drive through Fatihab, less glamorous but colourful, more like a suburb along a busy road. We no longer see only yellow taxis, but also small three-wheelers transporting people; goods are transported by donkey carts.

In Fatihab we turn off the main road and soon enough the tarmac ends, as do electricity poles and relative power cables. There are some more poles but no cables. The road has turned into a desert track. In the distance I see mud settlements reaching as far as the eye can see. We cannot see very far because of the *haboob*, which seems to be stronger here than in the centre of town. I ask my friend, "Who lives there?" He reminds me of the disappearance of the slums around Omdurman, perceived by me as "progress." He had asked, "Progress for whom?" an unusually cynical remark in Africa.

We are coming to the new home for people who lived in the slums when they were still called Internally Displaced People. There was talk in the early 1990s about more than 1.5 million IDPs in and around Khartoum. Maybe, this area can be called the fourth town of Khartoum.

The slums were an eyesore, and they attracted a lot of negative publicity for the government. Most of the people living there were from the South, many displaced by the war. Everybody could see that not much was done for them; they were left to the care of the Churches and some donor agencies. Their neighbours considered them to be thieves and criminals, accusing them of devaluing their property.

Around 1992 the government bulldozed these slums around Khartoum, loaded the people on trucks and dumped them here in the desert, some 25 km away from the centre of town where they had survived in the past. Some areas like Jabel Aulia are 40 km from town. The government did not want to recognize the term "Internally Displaced People" any longer. By removing them they did not have to face the problem.

Yesterday one of the displaced pastors from the South explained to me that the government had tried to do away with the term "Internally Displaced" before. When the war escalated in 1984/85 many people from the South fled to the North. One would expect the government to have had a policy to support these citizens, but the only apparent policy was to deny their existence. The government called the big crowds of displaced people coming in Khartoum, "Seasonal Migrant Labour." There was a national as well as an international outcry, which was still possible under the previous government. The new government for some years allowed at least NGOS to assist this people, but without making it easy for them. It limited food aid, saying that it only promoted food dependency and that it hindered the integration of the displaced in the national labour force. The pastor had explained that there was very little work for them, but more people looking for the few jobs would make labour even cheaper. He thinks that that was government policy.

When OLS accepted to supply food aid to the IDPs in the North, the government informed them that the only IDPs in the North were in the so called "peace villages." There were said to be sixty thousand of them. The more than a million people dumped here in the desert were nothing anymore, except perhaps "urban poor."

Southerners who have fled to Kenya or to Uganda have refugee status, which gives them the right to shelter, food, education, and some medical care. The status of the IDPs was not worth much before, apart from some relief from the Churches and from NGOS. But the government took away even that symbol of letting people know that somebody cared for them.

My friend and driver, a southerner himself, can get really emotional about a government that thinks it progress to sweep a problem under a carpet. He claims that more than 1.5 million people are trying to survive now here in the desert. Their shelters are built of mud or sun-dried bricks, made here on the spot. Some roofs collapsed during the rains of a few weeks ago. Another area seems to have been demolished and I am told that the government has decided that a new road has to be built there. As the land is not surveyed, in a way they all live here illegally as squatters with no rights. It all looks very drab. There is nothing colourful about this place, certainly not in a sandstorm. The only semi-permanent buildings giving colour are the mosques and a few churches. Also the Japanese who donated a few waterholes and water tanks let the people know, in big colourful letters, that the water tanks are a gift from the Japanese people.

How the people feel about living here is clear from the names which they have given to their settlements, I hear names like Mandela, Angola, Hillat Kusha (the garbage village). An even more telling name is Raas el Sheitan (Satan's skull) or Jabarona (we are forced), the name of the settlement we are going to.

We slow down for a very big bump in our track. It happens to be the pipeline through which the oil from the oilfields in the South is pumped to the refinery in Port Sudan. This oil seems to pay for a lot in Sudan, but not much is spent on these people here, who often have been driven away from their homes to clear the oilfields of people. Many of them live here where there are no jobs, hardly any education or health facilities. There is no running water nor electricity, and hardly any public transport.

We stop at a compound where people are celebrating a marriage. The happening is just as colourful as anywhere in the South of Sudan. It is obvious that most of the people living here are southerners. The ones who are celebrating the marriage are Dinkas. I have seen their home country in this season: it is lush green country full of cattle, with the children chasing birds away from the sorghum gardens getting ready for the harvest. What a contrast with this desert without any plants or animals except a few donkeys and some hairy goats that seem to live on the plastic bags

110

lying around. The donkeys pull the water carts, two barrels welded together fixed on a pair of wheels. These people seem to have lost everything, but they still dance.

I wonder how they survive here. My friend, who has worked with them for many years, tells me that most of them work in Khartoum and Omdurman, more than 25 km. away.

"Most of the families depend on the women," the one whose family we visit explains to me. She looks tired of the heavy burden she has to carry, or possibly the *haboob* gives her this tired look. She invites us to sit down in the courtyard around her house and sends one of her children to fetch a bottle of soda for the visitors. She obviously is a bit of a leader in a community of mainly women and children. It is clear to me that Kwaje, the name of our hostess, has explained the plight of these people to visitors before. In fairly good English, learned in primary school in the South, she quotes figures: "Nearly 70% of the adults here are women, many are widows or don't know where their men are. Others only know that their husbands are somewhere in the war. Life here is difficult enough for the women, but not at all easier for the men. The few who are here are jobless, and quite a few of them have a drinking problem. Since being pushed into the desert in 1991 we don't receive relief food; we cannot grow our own vegetables and we are too far away from the Nile for our men to go fishing." She nearly says that they had a good life in those terrible slums on the outskirts of Khartoum, the disappearance of which I had called progress.

My friend explains further. The women still play their traditional role in the family: looking after the children, providing food, collecting water, trying to keep the compound clean in a sandstorm.

But the few men here have no traditional tasks left, no cattle to be herded, no fishing, no hunting, no job. It is no use for them to sit and decide what to do; everything has been decided by the government without consulting them. They have really become nobodies, and it is not easy to keep your self-respect. I would

111

think that the men could be doing a bit more, but I also accept that it is not easy to change traditional roles. That cannot be done in a few years; it takes generations.

For some young Nuer there is an extra problem. One of the warlords from their home area, Commander Paulino Matiep, has rejoined the government and is now based in Khartoum. He comes now and again to press-gang some of the Nuer young men into his army. He takes them to the South to fight their Nuer brothers and sisters who are with the SPLA. He does not get many volunteers but the young men who try to escape are shot in the legs, or so I am told.

In spite of it all these people survive. The women leave very early in the morning towards Khartoum and Omdurman. They walk part of the way and the rest they travel by bus. Nearly half of what they earn, and at times more, goes into transport. It is often late when they come home again. I hear that only one or two percent of the people who live here enjoy a fixed salary. But it is the people who have no job who have to work really hard to make a living as casual labourers. Some make a risky living by illegal brewing. The greater the poverty the more people seem inclined to resort to alcohol to forget their misery.

A big feeding centre is being built, for parents to bring their children before they go to work. It is a Church project: the children get a meal a day and some people keep an eye on them so that they don't walk off into the desert and get lost while their mothers work in Omdurman or Khartoum. The relief received during the first few years for the children is diminishing, partly because the donor agencies get many other requests for assistance but especially because the government practically denies that internally displaced people exist.

The Churches have started some schools on their compounds, as have mosques. I am told that one has to become a Muslim to get free education in the Muslim School. With the Christians, school and church are on the same compound. The Churches could not afford to have separate compounds for school and church.

In general, Muslims and Christians in these areas live in peace, for in the desert they are all in the same predicament. But at an institutional level there is not much of a dialogue between Muslims and Christians. My friend asks: "How can there be dialogue between oppressor and oppressed?" Here they are all oppressed, Muslims and Christians. They are trying to survive in the desert and there is the dialogue of survival. They look to the Churches and the Mosque for support.

The only government office I see here is a police post. It is true that poverty and crime often go together, but so do poverty and sickness and I don't see any government clinics. Kwaje tells me that healthcare has been privatized in this country and people have to pay. This means that one cannot afford to be sick. Only Churches and some NGOS provide some primary health care.

Looking at all the misery, and knowing the South where most of these people come from, I wonder why they came to this place where they are not really wanted, except perhaps as cheap labour. The North seems to be enemy country for them. Even more I wonder why they haven't gone home after many years of such an experience. To me any life seems better than life here.

On the trip back to Khartoum I put this question to Elias, to whom we are giving a lift to Omdurman. He is well educated and politically aligned with the opposition to the present government. He tells me that at one time he was a seminarian in the South. He came to the conclusion that he might serve his people better as a politician than as a priest. Like so many Sudanese he is an expert on the history of his country. As a southerner he gives it a southern slant. Rather than answering my question he lectures me.

In the early 1960s, before the civil war really started, big floods struck the South. People lost cattle and crops and whole areas remained under water for months. Many Dinkas migrated to the North in the hope of making a living there. Elias raises his voice, nearly solemnly declaring that this was also the beginning of northern discrimination against southerners. These Dinkas had to take Arab names if they wanted a job, their children could only be enrolled in school if they adopted Arab/Muslim names. Elias explains that his people, who lived south of the Sudd, had been protected against slavery. But now they were almost made into slaves in Khartoum; at least they were not treated any better than slaves and often they were called slaves by their employers.

Other southerners came to the North after the Addis Ababa agreement, looking for work. He mentions the people of the Abyei, a part of the Kordofan that was not part of the South. The chief of these people had opted to remain with the North at independence in 1956. Again Elias raises his voice: "They chose to be part of the North but the Arabs never accepted them as northerners or as their equals. They did not develop the area and the people were forced to go as 'cheap labour' to the North, to agricultural projects or to Khartoum."

When the civil war started lots of southerners were displaced, as they still are today. People fled from attacks by both the SPLA and by government troops. Many fled to neighbouring countries, but just as many came to the North. I tell Elias that I have met them in Ethiopia, Kenya and Uganda and now here in their own country. He is not so sure that he can call the North his own country. He does not feel that he is treated as a fellow citizen by the Arabs.

Another group of displaced people are the people from the Nuba mountains, especially after some of their leaders, like Yousif Kuwa, joined the SPLA. Elias explains that most of the Nuba people are Muslim of African descent. Nevertheless the GOS declared the *jihad*, the holy war, against them. Many were killed, but many fled and try to survive here in the desert.

Another wave of displacement took place after the government lost ground to the SPLA towards the end of the Sadiq al Mahdi's government. When the government troops could not defeat the SPLA it reverted to the policy of arming all kind of militia groups to do the fighting for them. The best known are the Baggara militia who not only attacked and raided Dinka villages, but also killed many men, abducted the women and children and made the others flee their land. "Many of them are still here in the desert," Elias explains to me. He could go on lecturing me on the displaced of the Sudan since independence. But as we approach his home I remind him of the second half of my question: "Why don't they go home, wouldn't they be better off there?"

He becomes less eloquent. For Elias it is too early to answer. Some of the Nuba are going home to their Mountains after hearing that the ceasefire has been holding for a year. Security is very important for women and children. But few areas in the South can offer security without lasting peace. Another factor preventing the women going to the South with their children is the dearth of schools. Here the children are taught in Arabic; in the South they are taught in English and in the local languages.

Elias himself, and he is not the only one, considers trying to go to Egypt and from there to the US or Australia. In spite of the fact that he has had a good education he cannot get a good job, especially as a southerner who can't keep his mouth shut. He has considered going home to the South, but he is very doubtful whether the peace that at present is talked about will hold. Too many people seem to want war.

Elias is not the only educated southerner who is bitter and disillusioned, and who wants to leave but who is really needed when peace comes. I also realize that peace does not mean that South and North will be reconciled straight away. Some doubt whether they will ever be reconciled. Very little seems to be invested in reconciliation. The PR of this government towards the West is very good and many people in the West believe in the sincerity of the northern Arabs. But they have not succeeded in convincing the southerners here that they want peace, so as to share this beautiful country and their power and wealth with them.

Gabriel Cardinal Zubeir Wako, Archbishop of Khartoum, is a southerner who has lived in the North of Sudan for a long time. He cuts an impressive figure, a leader respected by many and feared by some. I share what I have seen and written with him. He knows about the Fourth Town. He has appointed some of his priests to care for the IDPs and he visits them regularly himself.

He doesn't think I exaggerate. On the contrary, he thinks my judgements too mild.

For years he has struggled to give education to the people in Jabarona and similar places. I hear from him the same things about education that Commander Yousif Kuwa of the Nuba Mountains told me years ago. The Cardinal has often told the IDPs that without education they will be used as slaves. He is inclined to think that what the government wants from the southerners is only cheap labour for industry and for the big agricultural projects around Khartoum. When the donor agencies were forbidden by the government to supply relief and to support education for the IDPs around Khartoum, this cardinal could not be stopped in his struggle for education. He started the "Salvage what can be salvaged" programme to give the displaced primary education. More than 40,000 children get education through this programme. Government education and its syllabus he considers as only a prolonged Quranic education, not really good enough to liberate people. Many donor agencies have told him that they cannot support this programme much longer. They have that power, and at times they think that the cardinal is a bit reckless to go on with this programme, but he considers it inhuman to stop it.

We talk about abductions and slavery. It is true, there are really many living in the Fourth Town. He looks at me and without the aid of figures and statistics he tells me about his celebrating Christmas in Jabarona a few years ago.

"It was a big celebration. Lots of people were there, as were the police to keep the peace. As I was speaking, a lorry load of people arrived. They were dropped on the church compound. We welcomed them, they were old men and women with few young children. They had not been worth wasting a bullet on, or being captured and kept as slaves. They told us how their village had been

116

attacked by the Baggara militia. The young warriors of their community had been shot before their eyes, the cattle had been driven away, the women and children had been captured and taken into slavery. They, the survivors, had fled northwards. On reaching Khartoum they had been loaded on the lorry and dumped here.

As they told their stories, a young girl saw a policeman with his gun and she thought she had to warn everybody. She trembled with fear. The people did not take much notice of her. As I was speaking she ran up to me, grabbed my hand and pointed at the policemen. But not even I could convince her that she had nothing to fear here from the police; she would not let go of my hand and she held on to me for safety for as long as I was there."

Feeling the fear of this girl and thinking of what she had gone through convinced the cardinal more of the truth of the stories people told than numbers and statistics that cannot be checked.

Back in my hotel in Khartoum I feel tired and dirty. I am glad that I can take a shower to wash off all the dust of the *haboob*. At the same time I am very conscious that the people in Jabarona haven't got that luxury. But the dust is minor dirt for these people. The humiliation, the discrimination, the verbal violence of being called a slave and being abused every day cannot be washed off that easily.

Abducted Slaves

Not knowing the misery (that awaits you at home),
makes you run back to the place
where they have sold you.

(Ugandan proverb)

Akech is one of the many thousands of Sudanese women. That is why she wonders that anybody would want to know about her when a teacher tells her that I am interested to hear her story to let the world know what is going on in Sudan.

We had been talking about the exploited displaced people from the South trying to survive here in the desert. Somebody pointed at Akech as a typical example of people who live in Jabarona on seeing her sitting in a bit of shade on the school compound. I had asked the teacher where all these people came from and how they landed here in Jabarona, which means "we are forced." She is sitting in the shade of one of the classrooms with her three children. I in no way want to put pressure on her but the teacher tells me that Akech knows that she is not forced in this case; she is only slightly shy. Her remarks about the world not being interested do not mean that she is not willing to talk.

I sit down with Akech and the teacher, who knows her well. Two of her children are here in the school. The teacher is our interpreter. He starts talking to her in Arabic, which I don't understand. They are both Dinka, but Akech is more used to Arabic than to her own Dinka language which she was not allowed to speak for many years. He explains to her that I am a Kawacha, a European, who has been working in Southern Sudan and who wants to know about the plight of southerners who have fled the war to find refuge in the North of Sudan. Akech protests that she hasn't really fled to this place. She didn't have much choice, for like most of the others she was forced.

Our dialogue proceeds slowly, as we have to talk through the teacher-interpreter. He prefers not to be mentioned by his real name and suggests Hassan. I am slightly surprised at his choosing a Muslim or Arab name, but he explains, smiling, that Muslims in this area seem to have more freedom of speech than Christians.

Akech is still fairly new here in Khartoum. She had hoped to find a better life for herself and her children, more human than the one she has led for the past 16 years. She hoped to find a new life with her own people. She comes from Aweil in South Sudan, near the border with the North.

The fact that the people who live there are Dinka is one of the reasons why they got into trouble. In the early years of the war SPLA and Dinka were synonymous for the government in the North. Killing a Dinka was like killing an SPLA rebel or supporter. The killing was not always done by the government soldiers. The government army delegated the fighting to local militias and paid them. They armed the Baggara and left them free to raid the Dinka areas. Even without permission, the raids did not stop. It gives very much the impression that the government condones the raids. Hassan tells me this before Akech gets a chance to tell me her story.

In 1986 or 1987, Akech is not sure, the Baggara raided her village. After surrounding it they started shooting, drove the cattle away and burned down the houses. There was great panic and chaos with much shooting.

Akech pauses for a short moment as if the worst is still to come. Then she says that her mother was shot on trying to run away from her burning house, looking for her children. Akech and her sister were hiding in the grass. After seeing her mother shot by the Baggara raiders they managed to flee and hide in a small bush. They stayed there till they heard the horses galloping away. Then they got up and saw that most of the huts of the village were still in flames. Many men had been shot; lots of women and children had been taken by the raiders. They were not the only survivors left behind, as others had also managed to hide. After the raiders left, the two girls took refuge in the house of their uncle, who lived on the outskirts of the village. His cattle had been taken together with the cattle of others but he still had his hut.

But this uncle did not feel safe anymore in the village. He did not have much reason to stay, as he did not have a family and most of the cattle had been raided. And he felt responsible for the safety of his two nieces.

At this point I venture to ask whether her father is still alive. Hassan and Akech look at each other with a faint smile, as if I had asked a stupid question. That was in fact the case. I was suggesting that her name was wrong, for "Akech" precisely means that her father was already dead at her birth. Hassan explains and I decide not to ask too many questions. The Africans are often forced to explain much to us, because although we know a lot, as often we understand very little.

With their uncle the two sisters waited a few days, after which he went to talk to other survivors before deciding that it was better to look for refuge in the North. Other people had fled to Ethiopia, but he preferred to stay in his own country as he knew that there were many Dinkas in the North, including from Aweil. They set out northwards. He knew about Khartoum but had never been there. He left his village in the early morning with his two nieces, walking in a general northern direction but not knowing how far it was and how long it would take.

Akech was eleven at that time and Hassan, who tells me more in English than Akech tells him in Arabic, figures out that the year was probably 1987. He explains that at the time the Umma party under Sadiq el Madhi had armed its followers, including the Baggara people, to fight the Dinka, who were seen as rebels to be eradicated. The Baggara raiders fought cheaply, as they did not draw a salary. Their only remuneration was the loot, a fairly common arrangement in the Sudan wars. Traditionally the loot is not only goods and cattle but also the women and children who can be abducted. Akech and her sister walked with their uncle from village to village towards the North, often spending the night with relatives near and distant. But even when not among their own people, they always found a place to sleep. Hospitality to travellers is not only a virtue but also a grave duty according to the Koran.

Unfortunately, in the second week of their journey, the village where they were staying for the night was raided one evening by the Baggara, and this time the sisters did not have time to flee or to hide. Their uncle was shot on trying to flee, but Hassan, who not only interprets but also makes running commentaries, explains that the uncle would probably have been shot, even if he had not tried to flee. The *murahileen,* as the Baggara raiders are often called, captured adult men, at times, instead of shooting them. Then they would cut their Achille's tendons so that they could not run away and were confined to work within the house or the courtyard.

While Akech continues her story I realize that in a matter of weeks she had seen her mother die and her uncle shot and she had nobody left except her sister. Still she tells this story in a very matter-of-fact way to Hassan. I wonder whether traumatized people unconsciously suppress their emotions so as not to get depressed, a luxury they cannot afford as they have to care for their children. Hassan already knows the story; for him Akech is one of many. I notice Akech watching me as Hassan speaks. I keep my emotions to myself while listening and taking notes.

The raiders, who came on horseback, put her in a sack like a load of grain. They hung her on the saddle and brought her and others to their camp, where they had more children, women and cattle. The raiders themselves had horses and camels. The captured women and children were tied to each other and a few days later they started walking towards Nyala, as she learned later. She lost sight of her sister. She wanted to give up, as she was tired and very afraid, but she saw that children who did not keep going got beaten. One who had tried to run away had been shot. One of the women to whom she was tied encouraged her and she kept going. It took many days, Akech does not remember how many, but in the end they reached Nyala in Western Darfur, the home of the Baggara raiders.

The whole village had gathered around the raiders admiring the loot: the cattle, the grain, the children and women. The loot was shared out to the different families of the raiders. Hassan tells me that they were treated like slaves; they had to do chores in and around the house and they had to cultivate the land. Akech says that at times they had to work in the fields of another family. They would not get paid; the family that had sent them would. For Hassan this last sentence makes a lot of difference, he adds, "They were not just 'treated' like slaves; they 'were' slaves." Hassan does not exactly define slavery, but for him the fact that the slave's labour is at the disposal of the slaveholder is an important aspect of real slavery. Akech confirms that they were called *abeed*, which means slaves.

I have noticed, in the last few days here in Khartoum, that southerners talk easier about slaves and slavery than people here in the North. Slave traders (or raiders) came from the North. Of course slavery is officially abolished and forbidden by law, but its practice has a long history in Sudan. For a long time the soldiers in the Egyptian army were slaves from the Sudan, especially from the Nuba Mountains, the Upper Blue Nile and the White Nile region. None of that stopped when European governments, at the beginning of the 19th century, started putting pressure on Egypt and Sudan to abolish slavery.

Quite some time after the slave trade had been officially abolished it was still the most lucrative trade in Sudan. Next to Zanzibar, Khartoum was in 1860 one of the biggest slave markets in the world, probably better organized than Zanzibar. It is thought that at least 5,000 traders were involved in a vast manhunt in the provinces of Bahr-el Ghazal, Darfur and Kordofan. This manhunt of course included women and children. An estimated half a million people were taken from the area and sold in Egypt and Turkey.

Even Gordon, the big opponent of the slave trade in the Sudan, who had been given full powers to suppress it, did not succeed in his campaign which he started on coming to Khartoum in 1877. At times he became desperate and at one point he wrote: "When you can get the ink that has soaked into the blotting paper out, then slavery will end in these lands."[6] Nearly ten years later, when he returned to Khartoum to fight the Mahdi, things were still very much the same. Gordon knew that he was fighting a losing battle but he could not surrender to the Mahdi because he knew that "the Mahdi tribesmen took no prisoners except women and children, all destined for slavery."[7]

125 years later I sit in the outskirts of Khartoum talking to a freed slave woman and not very much seems to have changed. But these days in Khartoum they are not called slaves; the term abductees and abduction are more common. I wonder whether that is so because slavery is forbidden by law and punishment for it could be quite hard. But the war seems to do away with all these niceties, apparently justifying a lot. Hassan confirms it. His Arab name allows him to be critical of the government, and he explains to me that the government refused even to discuss the issue of slavery with UNICEF, as it did not want to admit that slavery still exists in Sudan. In the end it was agreed to discuss abductions in a war situation over which the government claims to have no control. Hassan is disgusted with the hypocrisy of GOS.

I listen to Hassan and look at Akech. I don't know who of the two is more upset about not being paid for the work. I am aston-

6   Alan Moorehead, *The White Nile*, p 204.
7   Alan Moorehead, *The White Nile*, p 265.

ished at Akech's telling all this without showing much emotion, nearly accepting that things are what they are.

This changes when she starts talking of herself becoming a woman. "When I was discovered to be a woman new trouble started." She was given to an old man whose wife had died. She tried to resist but she was told: "Go to him or die. If you refuse him we will shoot you." She felt humiliated, like being raped. She strokes one of the girls' head while telling us that she became pregnant with this first daughter. Her second daughter was also fathered by that old man and she looks tenderly at her second daughter. She hated the old man but she loves his children with clear Arab features. They are beautiful children with Arabic names, but Akech has given them a Dinka name as well. She herself was given an Árab name. Although I am very interested in names in Africa I don't want to ask what it is, as she obviously does not want it. Her children speak Arabic. They have been told they are Arabs. All the women around her were Muslims. She does not think that she ever became a Muslim but she had to follow Muslim customs like Ramadhan.

The old man died and Akech felt relieved, but not for long. Soon after the funeral she was given to a paralytic who in no way could look after her and her two girls. Akech shows clearly how disgusted she is with how she was humiliated. After some time the cripple managed to get her pregnant and again it was a girl, the youngest child on her lap. The child, maybe 4 years old, looks at me as if wanting to say: "Sorry, it wasn't my fault, I couldn't help it." During our talk the three girls sit close to their mother. The older ones must understand what their mother is telling us. However I notice that Akech and Hassan at times talk in Dinka, a language forbidden to slaves. They would be beaten for using Dinka words.

For nearly fifteen years Akech lived as a slave with the Baggara people. She had to work hard in the house and in the fields. The children of the family for whom she worked went to school, but she and her daughters did not get any education. Her children were not even considered legal. They had no rights and could not inherit anything from their fathers, even though there was not much to inherit. Just when she, a little more than a year ago, had started to accept that this was her life and that life was miserable, some Dinka chiefs with some other people came to the village.

They were people from USAP. Hassan explains that it stands for "Union of Sudanese African Parties." This union, which opposes the present government, probably got involved in these matters to show to the world that slavery or abduction exists on a big scale in Sudan. They wanted to embarrass the government, which kept denying that slavery existed. They identified many abducted women and children to prove the government guilty. Partly under pressure from the UN, GOS had to do something to free abducted women and children.

Akech tells us that after a long meeting, she was called together with her masters. She was questioned by people from CEAWA (Commission for Eradication of Women and Children's Abduction). For once this organisation worked. She clearly expressed that she was not with these people out of her own free will, for often the masters claimed that these abducted women and children had freely come to them. Some of the Dinka chiefs had testified about the raid on Akech's village and the abduction could not be denied any longer.

The Baggara family with whom she had been all these years had realized that they had to let her go or risked being arrested. They had been hesitant to let her children go with her. They were the only people she truly loved, and she thought probably the only people who loved her. After prolonged negotiations the children were allowed to leave with her. She was given a blanket, a dress, and a few hundred dinar. She did not have anybody in Aweil to return to; the chiefs did not think that it was a safe area, and other Dinka people of CEAWA had told her that her sister was somewhere in Khartoum.

With the help of the network of CEAWA her sister was traced in Khartoum, and it was arranged that the two sisters would be reunited. Her sister had been able to flee with some other people soon after being captured years ago. Until 1992 she had lived near Omdurman; then she had been dumped in the desert with many others. Since then she had lived in Jabarona.

Like so many women, she tries to earn a living by brewing illegal liquor. She does not think it a very honourable thing to do, but here being restricted by circumstances leads to more evil than illegal brewing. People say, "A narrow basket bends the chicken's tail feathers." When her sister was told that Akech had been freed and was on her way to Khartoum she was happy, but also aware that she had little to offer.

She welcomed Akech and the three girls at night at the Khartoum railway station. People of CEAWA had paid for the taxi to her house, if one can call it that, here in Jabarona. Akech was shocked on seeing her new home in the morning when it became light. Her accommodation as a slave in Nyala had been better. Her sister did not have much to offer but she shared what she had, which is not much more than a roof that did not collapse during the last rains. "The family is an army, but it is your mother's child who is your real brother or sister," it is said in Africa. Akech's sister is not in a position to support her, but it never entered her mind to refuse to help her. It has taken time for them to get to know each other again after so many years.

Every day except Fridays, the Muslim holiday, Akech goes to Khartoum to earn little money by doing the laundry and cleaning the houses of a few Arab families. It is the same work she did as a slave, but the little she earns goes to her pocket instead of her master's. Her sister and her sister's children look after Akech's three daughters. Two of them go to school here, where Hassan has registered them without charging fees. Everybody is poor here, but some poor are indeed poorer than others. She makes enough money to feed her children but she cannot afford to get sick.

Akech looks at Hassan questioningly, wondering whether this is enough for the European who wants to know about southerners in

126

the North. She is nearly apologetic that she doesn't have a success story to tell.

I thank Akech for telling her story. I give Hassan a few thousand Dinars to give to Akech later. I don't want to give her the money now, for it might look as if I was paying her for her story.

Then out of nowhere, in this desert, somebody appears with a few Coca Cola bottles. They are called King Cola to make it sound less American. We have sat here for a long time, certainly too long for the three children who all this time have hardly said a word. Akech leaves for home to prepare some food for her children. We let her go.

I have many questions for Hassan about slavery and abductions. Hassan introduces me back to a community health worker with good contacts in UNICEF and CEAWA, who care for abductees in Khartoum. When we meet she is quite willing to tell me a bit more about the plight of these people in and around Khartoum. She is aware that some people got into trouble, even going to prison for accusing the government of supporting or at least condoning slavery. For only saying that there is slavery in Sudan they were charged with defaming the country. But that there is slavery in Sudan cannot any longer be denied. It is well documented by many organisations whose reports are usually denied by the government. It was an especially hard blow for the government when two university professors, who had set out to prove that there is no slavery in Sudan, came out with a most damning report about the inhuman trade of people and the killing of a thousand displaced people in the town of Dhien in 1987. Dr Suleiman Ali Baldo and Ushari Ahmed Mahmud wrote the book "The Dhien Massacre; Slavery in the Sudan." The fact that they are Arabs, teaching at a government university, made it only more embarrassing for the government. They were harassed, condemned and imprisoned.

I don't want this community worker to get into trouble. When I suggest not using her own name she suggests with a smile to be called Bakhita for this occasion. Saint Bakhita was the first Sudanese woman to be a canonised saint in the Catholic Church. She was sold as a slave six times, but after being freed she became a nun in Italy, and later a saint.

This newly-named Bakhita is in no way a slave but a free woman who fights for the rights of her people. She is a Dinka from Bahr el Ghazal but she grew up in Khartoum where she became a community health worker. She has been working in the camps for the displaced for years now. Through her work she got to know quite a lot of women and children who after being abducted had regained their freedom in one way or another. Often they were members of her own people in Bahr el Ghazal, who for Bakhita are her own brothers and sisters. She is the guardian of several of them living in Khartoum; she hasn't got children of her own. Bakhita is critical of the government, although she has been working for them. Being critical of one's employer doesn't help if you want to keep your job in Sudan. But keeping silent is not in her character.

We talk sitting under a big poster of the SCCs women group: "Remove the chains of oppression and the yoke of injustice" (Is 58:6). It could be Bakhita's coat of arms. She tells me about the history of slavery and abduction. For her the two terms are the same, although she is prepared to use the politically correct "abduction."

I tell her I met Akech and some other abducted children, most of them Dinka. I ask why so many of them are Dinka. She sighs deeply, "This war is ruining us. I wonder whether there will ever be enough healers to heal all the wounds of the different people of the Sudan. Of course slavery in Sudan is old, tension and quarrels over grazing territories are not new. In colonial days the borders between the Baggara and the Dinka were sharply demarcated down the middle of the Kiir River. There were disputes over grazing and fishing but the traditional chiefs could solve them in traditional ways."

She thinks that it was in 1985 when the war escalated and the government created new "Popular Defence Forces." They were given weapons and the freedom to kill, rape, enslave, occupy territories and expel the non-Arab people. An example of this is the Baggara militia forces, also called Murahileen, which seems to mean, "those who are constantly on the move," as they move fast on horses and camels. They came especially from the border area between North and South. They started burning down villages and abducting people in the way Akech and others have told me. First they ravaged Dinka country, the home of Bakhita and Akech, which they wanted as grazing ground for their cattle. They not only raided Northern Bahr el Ghazal, but also the Upper Nile as far as Malakal. Bakhita thinks that my impression is correct: most of the abductees are Dinka.

Bakhita knows the work of UNICEF and Save the Children Fund to free abducted people. Some people say that this is not good enough, as the government gets away with not being condemned for condoning slavery. But Bakhita claims it an achievement that the government at least acknowledges that people are being abducted during this war and has officially condemned this practice. She herself works with some government people for the eradication of the Abduction of Women and Children.

I ask her whether she knows the program of Christian Solidarity International to buy the freedom of slaves in the South. They are reported to have bought more than 35,000 slaves since 1995 at about $ 35 per slave, which in some areas in the South is the price of two goats. CSI has been heavily criticised and accused of promoting the slave trade instead of abolishing it. Bakhita has heard about it. She points out that the program has made the US especially aware that there is still slavery in Sudan. She says, "No, I would not support such an approach but I don't want to condemn it either. It would mean another war in Sudan on how slavery can truly be abolished. We have enough wars as it is." Buying slaves to free them somewhat legalises the trade. Abducted people should be freed because abduction is a crime. Bakhita does not understand that I seem to have questions only on how slaves should be freed and not about how freed slaves should be accompanied and find their way again in life. She has problems getting funds for her work: people like Akech need a lot of healing even after being freed. She knows many others besides Akech.

There is disagreement about the numbers of slaves in Sudan. Some claim that more than 200,000[8] have been taken into slavery during this war. Nobody really knows. Even when people don't deny having slaves, they will not tell how many, just as the Dinka people won't tell how many cows they own. Bakhita would not put the number higher than 15,000. The number goes up and down as new people are still abducted every day while others are released as Akech was, or manage to flee or are let free because they are no longer fit to work, discarded like a broken tool.

Bakhita does not agree with the government's claim that there is no slavery in Sudan, and that abductions are due to the war. She is more inclined to think that the war is a cover for the abductions, and that "abductees" is another name for slaves. Some have justified the abductions as an inevitable consequence of war, but for Bakhita slavery can never be justified, not even by changing its name. She does not believe that slavery will automatically disappear with peace, but she is convinced that it cannot be stopped with the war going on. It is obvious that some people want the war to continue precisely for that reason.

Many Sudanese say that the world has not done enough to eradicate slavery in the Sudan. Bakhita is not of those who want to blame it all on the outside world, which does not mean that the outside world cannot play a role. They can certainly play a better role than in the past. She is more inclined to agree with Abel Alier, southern lawyer and veteran politician, who in a speech commented on the text of Isaiah written on the poster in front of us; "Remove the chains of oppression and the yoke of injustice." Abel said, "The chains of oppression and the yoke of injustice must be removed by those who witness and experience both the chains and the yoke!"

Bakhita has witnessed a lot of oppression and injustice; Akech has experienced the chains and the yoke.

[8] Claimed by Sabit A. Alley in article; *Modern Day Slavery and Slave Trade in Sudan.*

Sr Paskwina

*"The young shoots of the arum-lily are planted slanting.
On striking roots they straighten up."*

(Ugandan proverb)

our gift came as a welcome encouragement towards continuing our struggle for the education of our children at St Kizito School, Isoke. We have 1,500 children now, what can we do? What will their future be without education? I cannot send them away. We are lucky that CRS helps us feed them. We have also started the school garden, but we have not been lucky with rain this year. We are still teaching under the trees; when it rains we teach in the dormitories, which are built of blocks and have good roofs. With the gift you sent us we will buy mats for the children to sleep on, because we don't have beds. I have told the children about Brother Patrick's gift. We thank him and pray for him."

The gift Sr Paskwina is writing about is $250, which I received from Br Patrick, a fellow Mill Hill missionary. The gift was meant for primary education in Sudan. Br Patrick was a missionary in South Sudan up to 1964, when he was expelled together with all the missionaries. He did leave Sudan but his heart stayed behind. Br Patrick hasn't really got money to give away. He is staying in an old people's home for missionaries, but he is not the kind to sit in his room all day. Next to the farm where he used to work when he was young, he sowed some seeds of trees. The place he had chosen carefully was an old manure pit. He grew very good seedlings, which he sold to the forest department. The $250 which he received for it he gave to me, after he once again told me about his stay in Lull, one of the early mission stations on the Nile, north of Malakal. There, more than 40 years ago, he had seen the importance of education. I sent the money to Sr Paskwina in South Sudan, where she is running a school in Isoke.

This Sr Paskwina is not young anymore, but far from thinking of retirement. She is a pioneer in many ways. She drives the diocesan administrator up the wall with the school accounts always in the red, but children are more important than accounts for her. She started without a budget and without plans. The school somehow "happened" to her. When people point out that that is not the way things get done these days, she smiles and says: "What to do? The children are there, how can I send them away?" The donors think, "What to do? We cannot stop her."

A few days ago we met at Ikotos, a neighbouring parish of Isoke. I asked her how she got involved in education. She is passionate about it. The long story starts with her own primary education in Isoke. In Africa there is time to listen to long stories. This is a shortened version. Sitting in the shade of a tree, Sr Paskwina tells me about her life.

"I was born in the neighbourhood of Isoke in 1949. At that time it was not common at all for my people to send girls to school. There is no need to go to school to bear children, to fetch water and firewood: that is how people thought when I was young. I had no ambition to go to school either. But my father was a soldier. He had been around during the war and had seen the world. He had seen educated women and was impressed. He was getting old and he wanted me, his youngest daughter, to be somebody. He decided to send me to the mission school in Isoke. My mother was not in favour and I did not like it either, one of the reasons being that there were very few girls. I ran away from school, but my father took me back. Not only my father encouraged me but also

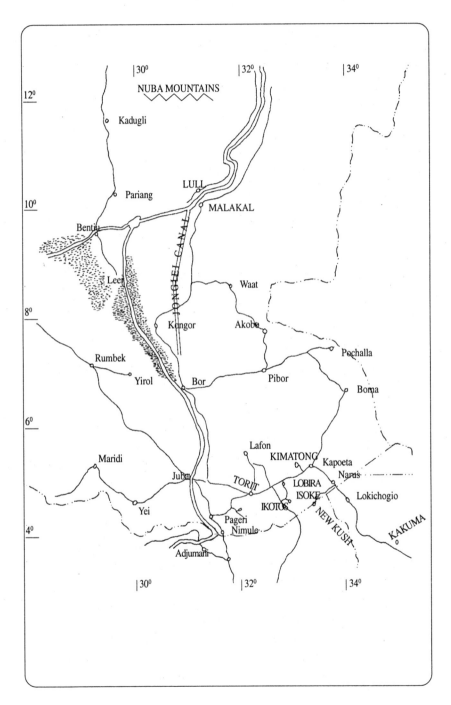

12°

|30°

NUBA MOUNTAINS

o Kadugli

LULL

o Pariang

10°

MALAKAL

Bentiu

Leer

8°

Kungor

Waat

Akobo

Rumbek

Pochalla

Yirol

Bor

Pibor

Boma

6°

Lafon

Maridi

KIMATONG

Kapoeta

Narus

Juba

TORIT

LOBIRA
ISOKE

Lokichogio

Yei

IKOTOS

NEW KUSH

KAKUMA

4°

Pageri
Nimule

Adjumani

|30°

|32°

|34°

133

the white Comboni sisters who taught at the school. I admired them and wondered whether I could not become a sister myself. When I told some friends they laughed, but when I told the sisters they did not think it a laughing matter. It was not easy to get my people's permission but in the end it was my father who agreed. I was a little over 14."

When I remark that 14 is a bit young to decide to be a sister she shrugs her shoulders: "Other girls were married off at that age." The year was 1962.

When the missionary sisters were expelled in 1964 the Sudanese sisters and novices could choose between going home and give up their vocation, or going to Uganda for further formation and training. Sr Paskwina knew that she wanted to be a sister and she went to Uganda. She would have liked to become a nurse after secondary school, but with no missionary teachers left in south Sudan the gaping need was for teachers. She obeyed Mother Superior and became a teacher, also for the blind, in Uganda. Of course she missed Sudan, but many of her people were refugees in Uganda during the first civil war, which lasted till 1972. She and many of her people were educated in Uganda. But Sr Paskwina wanted to teach her own people. In 1977 her superiors of the Sacred Heart Sisters asked her to go to Palotaka in South Sudan to teach in a mixed primary school. Palotaka is in Acholi land, but the Acholi and the Logire are neighbours and quite a few Logire children attended the Palotaka school. She did well, and in 1980 she was sent to the diocese of Malakal among the Shilluk. For a Logire like Sr Paskwina, the Shilluk were wild and primitive.

The Logire people had been wearing clothes for centuries whereas the Shilluk still did without them. But Sr Paskwina was happy to teach at the school in Lull, the place where Br Patrick and other colleagues of mine had worked till 1964. Some of the classrooms in which she taught had been built by Br Patrick. The fact that Br Patrick had worked in Lull had enhanced the value of the $250 for Sr Paskwina. It was from someone who knew Sudan, unlike most of the donors. She would invite the donors to "come and see" rather than asking her to sent long reports. She is willing and able to write these reports, of which she has written hundreds; for 12 years she was a member of the General Council of her congregation. For many years she worked also as the accountant. She was happy enough, but deep down she remained a teacher, at her happiest in a school. She missed school and often thought about her own people.

"It pained me that during the new war, starting in 1983, my own people were often near the front. In the 1990s many fled to Uganda away from the war, but also in order to get education for our children. So when I was asked to go as a teacher to the diocese of Torit I was only too ready. My superior asked me whether I was not afraid to go to a war zone. I was not. After all most of my life I have known war, I got nearly used to it. I did not get a feather bed job. I was asked to go to New Kush near Natinga, and start a school for the many displaced who had come a few years earlier from the refugee camps in Ethiopia. Many were Dinka. I started teaching again, under some trees as a classroom. I begged the World Food Programme for food for the children and I received food from CRS. The diocesan education coordinator found a few benefactors and the Kiltegan missionaries made a contribution. The financial administrator kept telling me not to spend money I did not have." But with a big smile she looks at me and says: "What to do? How could I send children away? Should I tell them to go to Kakuma away from their own country, while hearing all the time that refugees have it hard in Kakuma?"

She constructed simple classrooms and dormitories with the help of the people. By 1997, when trouble started between the local Didinga and the displaced Dinka the Sisters, with the help of the diocese of Torit and the Kiltegan missionaries had established quite a school for the children of both displaced and local people. The children got on very well with each other. But the trouble between Dinka soldiers and the local Didinga commanders became nasty and people got killed. The locals fled to the hills and the Sisters were accused of siding with them. After they were threatened with firearms Bishop Taban told them to withdraw. "What to do?" Sr Paskwina asks, "We had to obey and leave New Kush."

Sr Paskwina knows how to laugh at herself. She tells me that her fellow sisters and the Acholi people nicknamed her *akanyango,* an insect carrying all kinds of things on its back that it finds on the way. She thinks it does so for camouflage and survival.

"I carried what I could, but could not leave the orphans behind, who had nobody to go to. I took them with me. In February 2000 I arrived with them in Isoke, my home parish. The bishop told me to take a rest with my own people."

The Comboni Missionaries founded the Isoke Parish in 1926. Isoke is beautifully located between the mountains and two rivers. Here the missionaries had started two boarding schools; the people had come to value education. Because of the war the mission were closed between 1994 and 1998. But together with Sr Paskwina, Fr Joseph Mawa arrived. They waited for security to improve in New Kush, but when it did not happen they soon started to revive Isoke parish. The old school buildings for secondary and primary were in a bad state of repair and the zinc sheets on the roofs had been stolen. The locals accused GOS soldiers of ransacking the mission, but Sr Paskwina thinks the locals had a hand in stealing too.

Sr Paskwina did not have much of a rest. She started teaching her orphans under a tree. And since she was teaching in any case, it was hard to refuse the local children, who first looked on and then wanted to join. She considered it all part of her rest. She was glad to be with her own people, despite the unrest. There were many raids between neighbouring tribes and clans.

With Bishop Akio Mutek, Bishop Taban's auxiliary, Sr Paskwina and one of the priests started travelling from village to village talking about peace and education. Everybody wanted education for their children but it was difficult to send them to Isoke through the battle zone. People began realising that they could not raid each other's cattle when their children were in school together. Gradually Isoke became a kind of bridge for peace between the different villages in the area. Children come from far now, and the boarding schools started without proper planning. Sr Paskwina explains that she could not help it, it had to be done.

"One day a few relief lorries were going back from Kimotong in Buya land to Lokichogio in Kenya. The Kimotong people, who wanted education for their children, saw the empty lorries as an opportunity to send some of them to Kakuma to get education as refugees. Parents do get desperate during a war. They want a future for their children and there is not much of a future without education. The decision was a bit hasty but 55 children were loaded on the lorries. They arrived in Ikotos in the evening, but the authorities there were not so sure that this was a very good plan. They discussed it at length; they were afraid that the children would lose touch with the parents and that they would be picked up by the SPLA in Kakuma. Would they come back once educated? Too many of their people were already refugees in Uganda. Should they not try to educate the children here in Sudan? Who would look after these children? It is said that a child does not get enough to eat when the mother is not there. In the end the idea to send the children to Kakuma was dropped and the children were dropped at the Ikotos mission. The parish priest, Fr Arkangelo Lokoro, had also indicated that he was not in favour of sending the children to Uganda or Kenya. But he had neither school nor school building and suggested to drop them in Isoke where there were at least some school buildings and I Sr Akanyango, who had worked with displaced people certainly would accept."

The children arrived in Isoke and Sr Paskwina said: "What to do? We cannot send them away." That was the beginning of St Kizito Mixed Primary School. With the children from far away a simple boarding had to be started.

137

Sr Paskwina remembers very well the 29th June 2000, feast of Sts Peter and Paul, as the day she began St Kizito School. They could have been the patron saints but she selected St Kizito's name from among the Uganda Martyrs, of whom Kizito was the youngest, as the school's patron saint. After all he would understand how hard the life of the young can be in Africa. They started on the plot of the old girls' school, by now overgrown. Some trees provided shade for teaching and some wood for the roofs of the simple dormitories. Six dormitories were built for boys and two for girls.

Sr Paskwina always remembers her own struggle for education. She remembers the 55 boys from Buya in the lorry, but Mary Lodita has a special place in her heart.

"It was raining the day we started clearing the plot for the school. During the night the watchman knocked at the gate of our house. I was tired after a hard day's work and reluctant to get up, afraid of being asked to settle some quarrel or other between drunks. But I did get up and asked what they wanted. Two men had accompanied a girl. She spoke no language he knew. The men had said the girl wanted to join the school. I told him to tell the men to come back next day. The watchman pleaded, 'Sister, the girl needs help now. Come and see.' What to do? I went. She looked very tired; she wore a torn skirt and she had no luggage of any kind. In my simple Arabic I asked her name. 'Mary Lodita,' she answered. The men said the name was from Kimatong, which meant she was very far from home. I gave her a place to sleep. Next morning I called a boy from Kimatong who spoke a fair amount of English and he translated for me. She had tried to climb onto one of the Kakuma-bound relief lorries, but the grown-ups had thrown her out, saying that girls should not go to school. But Mary wanted to go to school, so as to be able later to administer medicine to her people. She had waited for another opportunity, but when no more lorries came she decided to go on her own, on foot. She looked no more than twelve or thirteen. She walked four days, following the main road in the direction the lorries with the boys had gone. Luckily she met the two men in Lobira, who were honey harvesters. Seeing how tired she was they offered her honey, but all she wanted was *moyo,* water. They took her home, gave her water and fed her. Then they asked her where she came from and where she was going to. She told them she hailed from Kimatong and was going to Isoke School. They listened in disbelief, but she sounded genuine, apparently knowing what she was up to. In the end they decided to walk with her to Isoke, where they arrived in the middle of the night."

"What to do?" Sr Paskwina was not going to send her away after she had walked four days to get to the school. Of course her parents had to be informed, and it would probably take some palaver before convincing them to let Mary stay in the school. But that worry was postponed. She asked one of the older girls to look after Mary, who was given a place in the classroom under the tree and another in the dormitory.

At first the children slept on the *dura*[9] sacking in which relief food had arrived, and which Akanyango Paskwina had not thrown away. Later, with Br Patrick's gift, locally made mats were bought, which were more like the beds they knew at home. At that time the school had no running water, but Isoke is located between the Iwali and the Lohinyang rivers from the mountains nearby. The children went to bathe in the Iwali where they fetched water for the school. The children are not spoiled. Sr Paskwina has authority in the school and they respect her. "A child is like a goat: both are herded by one with an authoritative voice" is a proverb she had heard from her own teachers in Uganda.

When it rained the teachers taught in the dormitories. Not even the government's air raids stopped the school. On hearing the droning of the Antonov they would run to the caves in the hills nearby. "God obviously put them there for our protection," Sr Paskwina says. But not only God protected her. One day there was not enough time to get to the caves. When the Antonov was overhead Sr Paskwina

---

[9]   *Dura* is the local name for sorghum.

told the girls to lie down, with her in their midst. Sr Paskwina is not exactly petite; some girls, thinking she would make an easy target for bombs, threw themselves on top of her to protect her. Nobody was hurt by the bombs, but Sr Paskwina was almost crushed by the girls. "Do you know, Fr Mathew, it was the biggest compliment my pupils ever paid to me."

NGOS and donor agencies working in the area came around to take a look. Sr Paskwina's smile told them the help she needed, but also that she was ready to struggle on without it. The NCA did a lot for education in this area before the war. They gave the school blankets, which was a great step forward as it can be cold at Isoke at night. CRS provides food to this day. But it is all rationed for so many children during term time. No food is provided for holiday time.

"Holiday time" is a figure of speech for Sr Paskwina. She is responsible for 270 orphans, whom she has to feed and clothe. Many of them came with her from New Kush camp for the displaced, but when people saw that Sr Paskwina cared for these children, many more came to her. At times one of the two parents is still alive but unable to look after the child anymore. The traditional system of looking after orphans within the clans has often collapsed because of too many displaced people. She pleaded with AVSI, a donor agency with the Italian Bishops Conference, and formed a committee of people with the task of making relatives understand that they have a role to play in supporting these children.

I ask her whether relatives do help. Some are very good, she says, but not all. And while laughing, she vents her anger against the aunt of one of the orphans.

"Both the parents of one of the girls died in the war. Natheyo was seven years old when she was left with her aunt. With many other children at home, her aunt did not care for her too well. A catechist, who was also a community leader, recommended Natheyo to me and we accepted her at the school. She did well, and when the holidays came we suggested that she would home to her aunt, also to show that education was good for girls. Natheyo convinced her aunt and did just that. After the holidays I asked after Natheyo, but nobody knew where she was. I saw one girl, however, wearing the clothes I had given Natheyo before she went home. Inquiring further, the girl told me she was the daughter of Natheyo's aunt, who wanted education for her daughter but who had kept Natheyo home as a house help. What to do? Natheyo had promoted education for girls but now she had lost her own chance. I went to the village and fetched her back. The woman, who by now valued education for girls, had her own daughter admitted to our school too."

At the end of some months the diocesan administrator can help, but there are months when Sr Paskwina is forced to tell the teachers she has no money to pay them in full, and her smile allows her to get away with it.

Without a plan and without a budget, Fr Mawa and Sister struggle on. The two bishops, Taban and Mutek, encourage them and prod the donors to go and take a look. The donors have helped to build classrooms and dormitories. Caritas France, CRS, NCA, Caritas Belgium, Cordaid and others have not let Sr Paskwina down. Caritas Switzerland is helping Fr Mawa to build a road. The children are growing up, so that they need separate compounds for boys and girls. A secondary section has started and it is now functioning. Sr Paskwina has her hands full with 1,500 children in St Kizito, of which some 1,300 are boarders. She is sorry that the girls are only some 300, but their number is increasing. Some of them hail from Uganda refugee camps, displaced from there by the LRA. They think Isoke is safer than Northern Uganda.

Besides running St Kizito she is also a member of the executive board of the secondary. Girls in secondary always go to her when in difficulty, as they often are.

Today a primary and secondary school can be seen and photographed in Isoke. Collateral effects of Sr Paskwina's work are not easily seen by outside observers, but the local people notice. They call her a woman of peace. Sr Paskwina laughs: "What to do?" She does indeed follow the peace talks going on, and she is glad of the ceasefire agreed between the government and the SPLA. Her worry is the LRA. True, they have not come to the school, but a few months ago they burned the lorry of the secondary on its way from Uganda. Last month three boys, who tried to go home for the Christmas holidays, were captured by the LRA and killed outright. "We need peace, a lasting peace," Sr Paskwina insists.

"What are you going to do when peace comes?" I ask. "I will dance and celebrate with the pupils," she answers. "With peace things will change. Schools will open in Torit, and many children will go home. Village day schools will open, which are better for the very young who need their parents."

I wonder aloud whether she will finally take the rest she came to Isoke for. She smiles, "You know, in the evenings I often look at the mountains around Isoke. I hear the drums and I see people dancing. They have fled into the mountains to be safe from the war. There are many children up there, but they don't go to school yet. When peace comes I will go and visit them just as we visited the villages with Bishop Akio. Then the school will be too small again. Now I don't have an office but only a small hut. We may have to build a whole office block. There won't be much rest, but what to do?"

A New Vision
at the New Site

"You are eating with one who can
pluck (plenty of) vegetables in her garden."

(Ugandan Proverb)

J t has rained a lot in the last few days. Everything looks green and lush on leaving Lokichogio in Kenya bound for South Sudan. The landscape is beautiful, green thorn bushes with green hills in the distance. There is a 20 kilometre stretch of no man's land ahead of us, separating not only Kenya from Sudan, but also the Toposa in Sudan from the Turkana in Kenya. They are related peoples who have been raiding each other's cattle for generations. The men wounded in these raids wear their scars with honour. Cattle were raided both ways; one can nearly say that the cattle stayed within the family. They had traditional ways of restoring peace. But these raids can no longer be seen as a cultural or traditional sport, since these days both sides have firearms instead of spears and arrows. Robbers in this area are also well armed. In some places bullets act as currency *in lieu* of money. Too many arms and too many people willing to use them are the reason why we travel with an armed escort to protect us from ambushes between Lokichogio and Nadapal. My driver, who works in the diocese of Torit, has been ambushed on this road a few months ago, and I myself survived an ambush here about ten years ago. So we are both a bit nervous and feel relieved on reaching Nadapal on the Sudan border. We are safe.

Nadapal isn't much of a place. It is a barrier across the road, a waterhole for neighbouring people and an office of the SRRA registering the cars coming into the Sudan. Here the SPLM is in charge. The current cease fire between the GOS and the SPLA means that we don't have to worry about being bombed by the Antonovs of the Sudan government.

Bishop Paride Taban is waiting for us to take us to the "New Site," where he had promised to take me. He is not the only one to greet us. There are lots of tired looking children sitting by the road with plastic bags. Some come running to the car asking whether we are going back to Kenya, hoping for a lift to Lokichogio. They tell us that they don't want to miss the roll call, or headcount as some call it, in Kakuma refugee camp in the north of Kenya. They certainly are disappointed to hear that we won't return to Kenya for a few days. Yesterday they could not travel because there were no cars going as the road had been made impassable by the rain.

I always feel uncomfortable with groups of begging children around me: they plead for help with their whole person. One even informs me that Jesus said that we should help the little ones. But there are times when we are as helpless as we feel. Moreover I don't understand why they are so desperate to get to the refugee camp in Kakuma, a place I would not go to if I had a choice.

As we drive from Nadapal towards Nagichot and Natinga, I ask why are hundreds of children trying to go to a refugee camp in Kenya during a cease fire, and with everybody saying that peace is around the corner. What are they fleeing from? Bishop Taban explains that they are not running away from Sudan. They are going back to Kakuma so as not to lose their chance of getting primary education and food rations from the UN. Many were refugees there with their parents, but a few months ago they fled back to Sudan because of trouble between the refugees and the local Turkana, who felt that they were just as poor as the refugees who lived on their land. The UN looks after the refugees but the Turkana feel that they had a right to their share. Fighting broke out, some people got killed and many fled back to Sudan, to become "displaced" instead of refugees. The worst is that there are not enough schools in South Sudan, and certainly not schools providing food for the pupils.

The Education Policy paper of the New Sudan reads, "Education shall be the right of every child regardless of ethnicity, culture, gender, religion and socio-economic status."[10] The next point says that education should be accessible to every citizen of the New Sudan, but this is not reality yet. Many children had fled to Kenya because of school facilities for refugees. The camp personnel are calling the roll of the refugees, to see who is still there. Absentees lose not only the right to the food rations but also their place in school. Of course it would be better if education was provided near home in Sudan, but that is a dream for the future. Reality is different. The bishop only hopes that the children will get a lift so as not to miss their place at the Kakuma camp school. He obviously contributes to education, but he does not agree with colonial educational policy, which left education in the hands of the Churches alone. But also SPLM, of course, can do very little without outside help.

We drive again through a beautiful landscape of thorn scrub. The hills look light blue in the distance, where we see a cloud build up for more rain. This does not worry Bishop Taban, our driver. He is used to bad roads, which have to be very bad indeed to prevent him from getting through.

At Kamuto (Toposa for "dark place") we turn off the main road and drive through a village among high trees. Not many people know the name Kamuto; the place is commonly known as the New Site, where Madam Rebecca de Mabior, wife of the Chairman of the SPLA started a new project to support some of the more vul-

[10]   2.1, under Goals and Guiding Principles of Education.

nerable victims of this long war. Here in the middle of nowhere we are warmly welcome in a well-designed conference centre. Our coming has not been announced, but that does not seem to matter. Bishop Taban is welcomed as an ambassador for education; they thank him for the way he has challenged them. He is obviously held here in high regard, and as I was with him they welcomed me too.

A group of teachers gathers around us, many not young anymore. They tell us about the place while we wait for Mr Deng Ariel, the director. They seem to be committed to education. Several of them did not have a chance to finish their university education, as the war broke out in 1983 and the education system in the South collapsed. They don't want this to happen to their children. They became teachers instead of lawyers, doctors or engineers as they had dreamed. A few of them had taught in the refugee camps in Ethiopia before 1991. We reminisce about their return to Sudan via Pochala, where I visited them.

We talk about Peace through Development, one of the slogans of the SPLM. They point out that you cannot have development without education, which they see as the cornerstone of it. An assessment of a few years ago makes it clear that only 30% of the children in Southern Sudan are registered in schools. This does not mean that 30% attend school. Many have been displaced again since registration; other schools have been closed because of lack of funds, of teachers of both. But interest in education in the SPLM, the community and the Churches remains strong.

Hoping for peace, the movement has thought quite a bit about the type of education they want for the people. As there is a lot of catching up after 20 years of war, they are thinking of adult education as well as of children. Their policy papers stress the humanities, science and technical subjects like carpentry, masonry, metal work, agriculture, etc. It is impossible to carry out this project in a war situation, but a start is being made here at the New Site.

One of the teachers stresses the importance of education for girls, and not only because the founder of this school is a woman, although they admit that she has been influential.

When Mr Deng Ariel arrives we are welcomed once more and he apologizes for the fact that Mrs Rebecca Nyandeng de Mabior is not present, as it is holiday time for the school. Madam Rebecca is in Nairobi looking after a sick relative. She is the motor behind the New Site. She is wife to Dr John Garang de Mabior, chairman and commander in chief of the SPLA. He is the soldier in the family, the military leader of the long civil war against GOS, although this past year he has spent more time talking peace than on the battlefield. Everybody is hoping that peace will be signed soon. But John Garang will not sign unless satisfied that it will be a just peace. "Better war than a bad peace," he maintains. His wife is trying to look after the most defenceless victims of that same war: widows, orphans and the disabled. Madam Rebecca and I talked after the sick relative, her father in fact, recovered. It was enough for me to call her over the phone and organise the meeting.

She really made me feel welcome. I was not conscious of talking to a First Lady, but to an ambassador for education on behalf of the New Sudan. She talks about the generation that had to do without education because of the war. "Fighting for our country also means fighting for education. Education is the key to a better life for our children." She is a mother herself, and her children are at school.

She has heard all the accusations about the use of child-soldiers, but explains that often they had no alternatives. Education offers other choices, and it does not mean only getting a diploma. Besides teaching subjects at the New Site, she is training people in agriculture, health and technical subjects, which she deems as important as mathematics. It is a pioneering work among the Toposa, who are not very interested in schools yet. Rebecca understands, because when she was young it was exactly the same among her own people, the Dinka. They became interested in education when realising that cattle could benefit from it too. She has some Toposa in her school now. She remembers how angry her uncles were when her father allowed her to go to school in Juba. "My father was a driver working with the Ministry of Education. He took me and my sister to school in Juba. My uncles, who were unhappy about it, took me home to Bor. But I struggled to get back to Juba and with my father's help I finished primary school. I started secondary, but got married before finishing it. I am lucky to have a husband who supported me in my struggle for education. When he went to the United States I went with him. We came back in 1982. When the war started in 1983 he encouraged me to go back to the States to finish my studies. But I refused, because I felt I had to be by his side in the struggle for a New Sudan. Travelling with him I have become more and more convinced of the importance of education. Education for the victims of this war is my contribution to the struggle."

That is it quite a contribution Mr Deng Ariel has explained to us. He is very much part of it and very willing to talk.

"The war has cost many lives of good men, committed to the struggle. They left behind widows and children. Many children have been orphaned by the war, losing both parents. We all know about the bombing raids and the mines that left many dead. Many survivors will be handicapped for the rest of their lives. Madam Rebecca did not want to make beggars of these people. She tried to give them back their self-respect by making them self-supporting with income generating activities."

They began with some grinding mills in New Kush, Nitinga and Narus, plus a cooperative shop. They tried tailoring, sending some women to Nairobi to be trained. Mr Deng is willing to admit that it all failed, not because somebody stole the money but because they just lacked managerial skills. Most of the widows had little or no education and so did the orphans. Madam Rebecca herself did not have a chance to finish her formal education because of the war, but she got educated by the journeys she made with her husband

and by what she saw happening around her. When I talked to her she said, "I got my education at the university of life." Agreeing with many church leaders, she stressed that the victims of war should not be left to foreign NGOS.

Mrs Rebecca started an NGO to enable widows, orphans and the disabled to generate incomes for themselves, for a quick re-integration into society. The NGO was started in 1995 and was called WODRANS (Widows, Orphans and the Disabled Rehabilita-tion of the New Sudan). New NGOS are mushrooming in Sudan and it is not always easy to see which of these are poisonous and which are edible by the people. In the case of WODRANS the first effort was not a great success apart from the fact that Madam Rebecca and her team realised that education and capacity building were priorities. Of course it is a credit when people can learn from their mistakes. They evaluated WODRANS and the new emphasis seemed to be education. Their target group remained the same: widows, orphans and the disabled. Mr Deng Ariel shows me the ambitious-sounding mission statement of WODRANS:

"WODRANS works with the widows, orphans and the disabled whose survival, protection and development have been jeopard-ized by historical oppression and neglect, and by the present com-plex war, disease and recurrent famine. In its quest to meet the needs of these vulnerable groups, WODRANS aims to relieve dis-tress and rehabilitate; enhance and protect dignity; promote self-reliance; alleviate poverty; reintegrate and seek to ensure a return to normal living and full participation of those groups in the devel-opment and evolution of the New Sudan."

A mission statement is one thing, but to turn it into reality is another, as I know well in my own society. The team discussed the necessary strategies to achieve it.

They started a rehabilitation program to encourage self esteem and self-importance among widows, orphans and the disabled. One important way was to help them to earn a living by some income generating project. They started training people in tailoring, carpentry, blacksmithing and other production activities. The importance of agriculture was stressed so as not to remain dependent on relief food. Large parts of South Sudan are very fertile. But the basic strategy to achieve the mission of WODRANS is education, formal and informal.

Mr Deng has certainly the gift to sell this project to visitors, but I venture to ask what is being achieved, trying not to sound sceptical. The headmaster of the school is called and he shows us around with some of the teachers. I am impressed.

The school is not just a primary school. In January 2000 Madam Rebecca opened the "Nakwatom Heritage Academy" with boarding and counselling facilities to give the pupils a better future. At that time they had 240 orphans and other unlucky children. They were difficult to select, as 880 pupils had applied for the 240 places. Selection had not been easy. They had decided that at least 50% should be girls, and 60% of the available places should go to orphans. Thirty places were given to students from the Nuba Mountains at the request of Commander Abdel Aziz, the successor of Yousif Kuwa in the Nuba Mountains. He is just as convinced of the importance of education as Commander Yousif Kuwa Mekki was and he encouraged Madam Rebecca not to give up when the going was getting difficult. They wanted to give the local Toposa and neighbouring tribes a chance, but that was probably still too early. Some came but they left soon. Off late a few have come again and they are staying, it is a slow process. The school has by now more than 500 pupils.

The classes, dormitories and the dining hall are permanent buildings, very exceptional in Southern Sudan. But Madam Rebecca is herself very exceptional and she thinks that these war victims deserve the best. Of course a lot of bush and trees had to be cleared to put up the buildings, but enough trees have been left to provide camouflage for the buildings so that they offer no easy target from the air. The big water tank is hidden among the biggest trees on the compound.

It is holiday time and most of the pupils have gone home. Only the Nuba students are at school, since they can only reach home by plane, a luxury which the school cannot afford often. We talk to some of them. They consider themselves lucky to be here, but they miss home. But they have been promised that by the end of the year they will be flown home for the holidays.

Nakwatom, the name of the place where the school has been built, is Toposa for "the place of white elephants." I am glad that that the academy is not a white elephant. Funding it has not been easy. Being the wife of Dr John Garang may sound as a qualification for easy funding, but the fact has also disadvantages. People and organisations don't want to give the impression that they are supporting the SPLA. Madam Rebecca and her team have invested in making the project self-supporting. The conference centre has been built to generate income for the school. Most of the builders of the school-cum-conference centre have been trained here on the spot. It is a luxurious place for the South of Sudan, with self-contained rooms and flush toilets, whereas in most other places you are lucky to find a pit latrine. This conference centre is rented out to NGOS like the UN or the WFP to hold their conferences in Sudan instead of Nairobi. Of course it is also an opportunity to show their personnel what is happening here. Some have been helpful in providing food for the school, but that is a temporary arrangement. At the moment plans are being worked out for a school farm to grow their own food. Madam Rebecca is grateful for all the support of people and organisations, but she tells me that she keeps praying to God to show her what should be the next step.

There are also dreams for producing more than what the school needs. The local Toposa are not cultivators, but the war has displaced many people. Nomads and tillers of the soil need each other.

After signing the visitors' book, commenting how impressed we were, we drive back to Narus, hoping to escape the rain pouring from the dark clouds around us. We don't quite manage. Close to

Torit it starts pouring, but we have nothing to fear. We have a roof above our heads and we know that the road ahead is good enough not to get stuck. On entering Torit we see that lots of children are less lucky. They huddle under some trees in pieces of plastic, still hoping for a lift to Kenya. I wonder whether things will change for them when peace comes, education for all and not only for ex-child-soldiers, ex-slaves, war orphans or the handicapped.

I have asked Madam Rebecca about her expectations. Her quick answer shows that she has been asked this question before. "We take things as they come. Peace is not final. It is not an end but a beginning. The big change I am looking forward to is the quietness following the laying down of arms. Without endless battles, and no longer bombing raids, people will be able to travel again. There will be new challenges and we have to set our priorities right. There are health, infrastructure, the economy, the returnees and so many other issues. I know that education is a priority. When peace comes we shall celebrate it, but it will not be a time to sit down. We will tie our shoelaces and start with real work."

Madam Rebecca, Bishop Taban and I hope that then the time will come when children will not have to flee any longer to other countries to get a place in school.

Lost Ben Yak

*"A child given to somebody else to be brought up,
dies in peace only at home."*

(Ugandan proverb)

Before we met in Tucson, Arizona, USA, I knew about Ben Yak's life. He had written it down for some church personnel who had taken a special interest in the tribe of the lost boys of Sudan, as they have been dubbed in the USA. He was getting inculturated in the American way of life, learning about computers. When I wrote to his guardian that I would like to meet some of the Sudanese young men who had gone to the US she wrote back that she would inform a certain Ben Yak. A few days later I received an e-mail from him with the story of his life. He had written it down in the Kakuma camp for the UNHCR on being selected to go to the USA with a few thousand other boys. Part of his introduction to the American way of life had been learning how to handle a computer and using the Internet. His mailing the story to me meant that he was progressing. I thanked him and told him that I hoped to meet when I would come to the US. He asked me for news about his parents, but I could not get any, as I was in Holland preparing to go to the USA with two Sudanese bishops.

We met this morning in the community hall in Tucson. He greeted me as a long lost friend although we had never met before. We were of course acquainted through our correspondence. His first question was about news from Gogrial. He was visibly disappointed at my having no news of his people. After all the years away from home he is still very much aware that he had to flee without being able to say goodbye. I remembered his story as being much the same as those of thousands of other boys. But the beginning is slightly different. He left home without a chance to say goodbye. He remembers leaving home as "The Narrow Escape," the title of the story he sent me.

"The Narrow Escape took place when I was about ten. I left Gogrial, my home town in Southern Sudan, in 1987. I was separated from my parents when a band of Arab militiamen invaded our village. At the time of the attack, I was tending my father's cattle in the grazing field some fifteen miles away from the village. In a surprise attack, I heard the report of a gun and saw four Arabs in green khaki uniform with guns and swords in the middle of the cattle.

I was sitting in tall grass, where I hid to avoid being kidnapped by the attackers. Shortly the four started driving the herd towards the north. I hurriedly got up and ran home to tell the news, but I saw huge smoke billowing from the village. On the way home, I met two fellow villagers running away from the scene. Unfortunately one of the men was shot dead before me as they were attempting to prevent me from going back into the village. I laid flat on the ground, because the bullets whined very close overhead. I thought deep in my heart it was the end of my life. I spent some helpless minutes rolling and crawling on the ground to find a safe place.

Despite the incident I made it to the village, but I found it absolutely empty. More scared, I saw three people lying on the ground in a pool of blood; the huts were burning and collapsing around me. Despairing, I quickly ran across the village into the dense and dark forest, knowing nothing about my parents and other relatives. It was about five o'clock in the evening. Many women and children were abducted and taken into slavery to the North, the basis of Sudanese Islam. The men were shot dead or slaughtered as a means of depopulating the South.

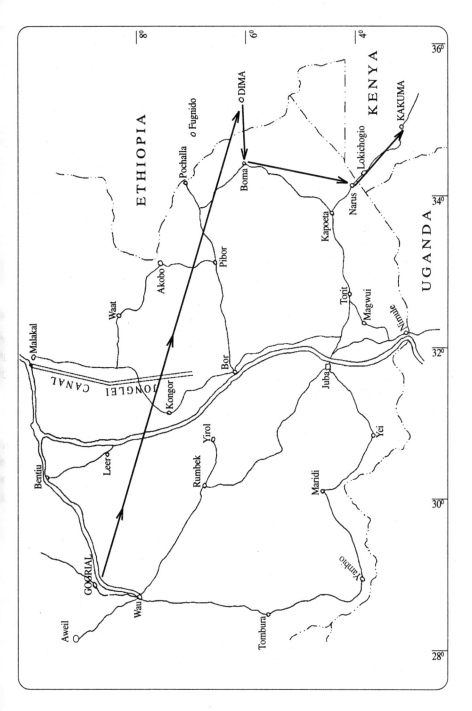

In the forest I climbed up a tree to spend the night, since it was dark and I feared wild animals, especially lions. It was a sleepless and gloomy night which I will never forget. By dawn I heard some people speaking my language. Peeking through the leaves, I saw them coming towards the tree. But I was really in a terrific dilemma: whether to give myself away to the group or to keep silent until they left. In the end I gained the courage to greet them, for they were talking about the day's ordeal. On hearing my feeble greeting voice the group at first seemed very scared and about to run away. But they soon realised I was only a small boy and one of their own, because we spoke the same language. They calmed down and welcomed me. I climbed down the tree. One sympathetic man gave me some water to drink since my throat was so dry that I could not talk normally. We rested for a few minutes and they told me to follow the group. I did not know where we were going.

After two days walking barefoot with the group, we fell into an ambush of Arab soldiers. The soldiers fired into the group, leaving many dead. The enemy kept firing, bullets whizzed and skimmed all over. In a panic, we ran in separate directions. It took hours before we joined again.

We walked on, reaching the Nile after one full month of travelling. We camped for two weeks on the banks of the world's longest river. We were often attacked by swarms of mosquitoes, which breed along the Nile. I swam across the Nile with many others, helped by bundles of papyrus, which is very abundant on the Nile. While crossing the river, some were swept away by the strong current. We were also attacked by aggressive crocodiles, which killed some people. Luckily I made it across.

After crossing the river, I was told that we were going to cross the Sahara desert to Ethiopia, which would take another three months. So we started our journey across the long and hostile desert. I did not carry heavy loads as I was young, ten or eleven years old. I had only a small stick meant for protection. We encountered many problems in the desert. First it was very dry and windy during daytime; so we were always thirsty. We tried to lick the dew on the shrubs in the morning. But it did not at all quench the thirst. Then there was hunger, since we did not have any food. Some young people were unable to continue, as they ran out of energy to keep walking.

They were in total despair. They lay in the scrub as the only peaceful way to die rather than suffer a prolonged, traumatizing, exhausting journey through the desert. We also ate tree leaves, but it was hard to get edible leaves because of the harsh climatic conditions. Occasionally we killed gazelle for meat; but it was quite hard to capture them as they ran away from people. Some wild animals like rhino and buffalo were very dangerous, since they could not be killed with ordinary spears. So we hid whenever coming across one, and whoever was closest would climb up the nearest tree for protection if it became aggressive. The meat and leaves were inadequate to sustain life. Hence, some people starved to death and others died of dehydration. I personally saw four age mates die. There were also angry snakes that bit many of our group. Some of us died of snake bite, because there was no treatment.

I reached Dima Camp in Ethiopia alive but I had to be hospitalised for several weeks for chronic malaria and various deficiency diseases. I did recover and ended up spending four years in the country. In Dima Camp there was enough food, but no education or medical attention, at least not enough. For education, I used to sharpen some pieces of charcoal to use as pencils for writing notes. Also, I peeled a piece of cardboard to use as exercise book for note keeping in my level one class. I started school in 1990, when I began to learn the English alphabet. Socially, we did work hand in hand taking care of ourselves. We could build our own houses using grass for thatching and mud for the walls. We cooked and did the laundry for ourselves. We did get supplies of blankets, sleeping mats and clothes from the United Nations High Commission for Refugees (UNHCR). We played some games for fun, like soccer and English word spelling. We swam in the nearby river during the summer season.

In 1991 I fled from Ethiopia back to Sudan with many other refugees since the country of Ethiopia plunged itself into civil war, and the incoming rebels were clearing out refugee camps. Thousands of refugees were killed by the rebels and many others drowned in the Gilo, Jael el Righf rivers. The new camp was established at the Sudan-Ethiopia border. But there was no food. We spent two months wandering in the forest looking for wild honey and animals for survival. If we did not find anything, we would cook leaves to eat in order to survive. In the forest we could stay in small groups, then we would end up back in the camp."

Ben Yak describes his journey further. It resembles the story of Dut and others, with one difference: Ben Yak managed to escape the actual fighting experience of so many others. Or he did not, but he did not think it wise to write about that either to the UNHCR or to me, especially as the Dinka boys in Kakuma were often accused of being SPLA soldiers. For nine years he lived in Kakuma refugee camp, getting as much education as he could, while many of his colleagues were struggling in Uganda. In the end his sticking it out in Kakuma seemed to pay off. Ben Yak writes:

"In 1998 we were approached by the UNHCR and asked to write our life history in an attempt to start a refugee resettlement program in the United States. We then went through a series of interviews to screen those who would come to the United States. We were required to have a medical check-up after passing the final interview with Immigration and Naturalization Services. In November 2000, I got a letter of approval for refugee status in the United States. On February 8, 2001 my name appeared on the notice board for the flight scheduled for February 12, 2001. I arrived in the United States on February 14, 2001, St Valentine's Day."

Today he has come from Phoenix with a bus load of Sudanese young men to meet Bishop Paride Taban and me. We celebrated the Eucharist together in the church of a Catholic parish. We used English, but most of the songs were composed during the war in

Sudan. Many young men are Protestants, and they taught their songs to the Catholics in the refugee camps where they were staying. After their Ethiopia experience they all felt at home. Bishop Taban presided. They are more ecumenical than the society in which they live here in the US. After the service there were speeches. We watched a few videos about Sudan and I am now sitting at the back of the hall with Ben Yak and a few other young men. The bishop has gone to baptise a few Sudanese babies born here in the US. The fact that they were born here does not make them any less Sudanese, and the parents find it important that they be baptised into that Sudanese community. The fact that they are learning the American ways does not mean that they feel that they are American, here they feel themselves even more Sudanese than at home.

Most of the young men with whom I sit at table have been in the US a bit more than a year. Ben Yak has been here longer. They are smartly dressed in casual clothes of the latest fashion.

They have more questions about home than I can answer. They have heard about the peace talks in Machakos and Naivasha. Do I believe that these talks will bring peace? I am somewhat sceptical, but it is at least an opportunity, I suggest. They conclude that I, who sound optimistic, don't know the Arabs. I should know they know the Arabs better than I do. We talk about the battles around Torit, which was captured by the SPLA and which the government was trying to retake. Some of them know the place too well as they were there defending Torit in 1992. They lost that battle, and GOS captured the town after being in the hands of the SPLA a few years. They inquire about Fr Tim, who was with them in the Kakuma refugee camp. I know Fr Tim, and tell them that he is working in Sudan in Nanyankachor. They are trying to figure out who else I must know from whom they have not heard anything since their arrival in the US.

It takes some time before I turn the tables and ask them some questions about their journey after Kakuma and about their stay in the US. Were they prepared for what was coming? They giggled about their cultural orientation in Kakuma. Yes they were told about the US. They were told about the cold. They were even given ice cubes to feel what cold felt like. Kuek said he did not know why it was called "cold" because it burned in his hand. Then they were brought to Nairobi a day before flying to the US. They laugh on remembering the moving staircases in Yaya centre, which they were afraid to step on. Now they know that they are called escalators and they are nearly disappointed when there are no escalators and the have to use staircases. They have learned fast in this new land. Of course they had seen aircraft before, but they always had to figure out whether they were relief planes or bombers. They travelled several days by plane before arriving in the Arizona desert. They tell me they were even in my country, which one of them calls Amsterdam.

There was a lot to learn: how to use a flush toilet, an electric stove, how to cross the road where the throngs of cars reminded them of a stampeding herd of cattle. Some of them, here in Tucson, were learning computers at the social centre of the Church of the Brethren. They felt very welcome. The Churches were helpful but they also mention the Jewish Family and Children Services. The US government had been very helpful, at least for the first eight months. Via the Refugee Resettlement Programme they received $ 456 a month, and it was a lot easier to get a sponsorship for education here than in Kakuma. Many of them sent a good chunk of their money to relatives and friends in Kakuma. Many of them are trying to stand on their own feet, get their green card and go home to bring a wife from home. Some have even brought their own mother to look after the children but also not to loose their own culture.

Others, unfortunately, remain very dependent, perhaps due to the fact that they have been many years refugees in Ethiopia and Kenya, where they always were catered for. People react differently to being helped. Bishop Taban told them this morning the story of the good king.

"This king cared for the people. If people were sick he would support them, the poor could rely on his support. For the unedu-

160

cated he built schools, the unemployed he tried to give work and he challenged his people to care for each other as he cared for them. The people loved this king. But even good kings die and so did this king. The whole nation came to the funeral and mourned their king. But there were two groups who had come. The first group thanked God for the life of the king who had shown them the way. They prayed to God to reward the king with heaven. They went home and started working knowing that now they had to get on without the king.

The second group lamented at the funeral that now they had nobody anymore who would help them. And even after the funeral they kept coming to the widow begging for help. However the widow only could show them the grave and explained once more that the king was dead." The boys listened to this story, smiled at one another and remained silent. It is quite a challenge for them.

Later I ask Ben Yak about Phoenix. He is happy that the stories about the terrible cold are not true. The climate in Arizona is nearly as hot as in Sudan. But one of them recently came from Chicago, where he felt cold and saw ice. Some fishermen had even built small houses on the ice. Some Sudanese arrived in Phoenix eight years ago and by now they have made it in the US. They try to counsel the newcomers. They have overcome their early fears and they laugh and joke about it now. Doors seemed bewitched, opening before you touched them and you could not see who opened them. We have heard the same stories in other places. The men and a few women whom we meet here are not the only "lost boys" from Sudan who have come to the US in the last few years. We met more of them in New York, Washington, Chicago, Tucson and San Francisco and we would have met them in many other places, had we had the time to go there.

They have accepted to be called "lost boys" if that term brought possibilities and money for them to get to the USA. But one of them wonders how his future wife and future son will feel when they will be called wife and son of a lost boy.

161

A few days ago a lady of the Episcopalian Church in Chicago, who had visited Kakuma, told me that the United States agreed last year to resettle about 3,600 of unaccompanied minors who had travelled for years to get some education. There were very few girls among them, but then very few girls had had enough education for further studies in the US.

It is all part of a resettlement program of the UNHCR. The US government is involved but the Churches have also been very supportive. The American community has been generous, but some are wondering what is enough and when the need will end. These questions we hear in a church hall where we gather with the Church community trying to support a group of so called "lost boys." It is obvious that the Americans themselves are somewhat at a loss. They are trying to support the *lost boys* and the more they give the more the boys seem to send home. Also State Department people seem astonished that the Sudanese are not more grateful for all the material help they give. Listening to them I wonder whether we in the West have become so poor that we only can give money.

I am the last one to say that money is not needed, but solidarity is a lot more than just giving money. They wonder what their role is and look at Bishop Taban for an answer. Instead of abstractions they get a story about a Sudanese father and his three sons.

"The father felt that his end was coming. He had lost his wife in the war, and many of his cattle had died or had been raided. With less than 20 cows left he was a poor man. Before he died he told his sons to keep peace among themselves and share his herd in such a way that each would receive according to what he had contributed. The eldest son, who had herded the cows longest, who had defended the herd in many raids, who never had gone to school, should get half the herd; that is what the father decided. The second son had not been with the cattle so long, a few cows had even been sold to pay for his school fees and the father decided that it would be fair for

162

him to get one third of the herd. The youngest had only herded goats and sheep before he went to school. Perhaps he was too young to get cows, but the father wanted him to have his share too, and he told the two elder brothers to give him one ninth of the herd and to keep the peace. And he died.

After the funeral the three brothers sat together to divide the herd. It was not an easy task after counting the 17 animals of the herd. Half, one third and one ninth of the herd meant cutting up and slaughtering cows. That would have been all right had they been butchers, but they were cattle people and each wanted to build up a new herd. What to do? As there was no mother to advise them they went to an old wise woman. She was poorer than they; she had only one cow, but she had wisdom. She took the one cow and added it to the herd of the three brothers, who had now 18 cows and dividing now became easy. The eldest got half the herd: nine cows; the second son got one third, or six cows, and the third son got one ninth and was happy with his two cows. Nine and six and two is seventeen and the brothers saw that one cow was left over, which they gratefully brought back to the wise old woman. They told her they would never forget her wisdom and help. Only some time later the old woman discovered that her cow became pregnant in the short time which it spent in the herd of 17 heads of cattle."

Bishop Taban wonders whether the US would play the role of the old lady. Also that is quite a challenge.

Blind Trust

"When God gives you a load,
He also gives you a soft pad to carry it."

(Dangme proverb)

The better I get to know the situation in Sudan the more I am amazed that people don't give up hope. Often western people like me wonder how can any one struggle on after more than 20 years of war. I cannot answer that question. I don't even think I have a right to answer it on behalf of the Sudanese. I remember though putting this very question to bishop Taban some years ago.

We were driving through the endless plains of Southern Sudan talking about the similarly endless war. We talked about the plight of the ordinary people who suffer most, women and children. Bishop Paride Taban, our host and driver, had just told me and some visitors from Europe how whole areas in the Upper Nile, where oil had been discovered, were being cleared of people. First the areas were bombed to scare the people away, turning many of them into refugees. Then the government sent helicopter gunships to kill those courageous enough to stay. We know that the oil revenues are used to fuel the war. The situation looks hopeless to me.

The bishop, about to travel to Europe, asked me what I considered most important for him to tell my compatriots. I said that there was some awareness about the war, the refugees, the war children, the hunger; and also that it never stops. To us the situation looks hopeless; we don't see any light at the end of the tunnel. Has he any hope? Does he see any light at the end of the tunnel?

The bishop, who is a worried but not desperate man, is silent for a moment as he manoeuvres the car through a dry river bed. He is thinking. Back on the road he says: "So, they want to know why we don't give up hope and whether we see any glimmer of light in the situation in Sudan?" I said, "Yes, many of my compatriots would certainly like to hear his answer to the question." He chuckled and asked: "Do you know the story of the mayor who had to get to the town hall during a tornado?" I do, but I always say I don't, because he tells his stories ever differently, depending on the audience.

The mayor was to lead the tornado crisis team. He opened the door of his house but could not see his way because of the storm, the rain and the wind. There were no cars on the road, as the road was blocked with trees and fallen branches. He closed the door again, but he had to get to the city hall. After all he was the mayor and his leadership was needed in the crisis. He opened the door again, but he saw more trees uprooted and the streetlights out, but he saw someone moving in the street. He could not see whether it was a man or a woman, but he shouted: "Where are you going, can you help me?" The figure said: "Where do you want to go?" "To the city hall, I have to lead the people through this crisis," the mayor shouted in the hope of being heard in the storm. The figure took him by the hand and led him through the streets. The figure guided his hand to feel where trees were lying across the road and he helped him to climb over them; he made him hold on to the walls and helped him through the ditches. They felt their way, the mayor holding on to the figure who seemed to know what he was doing. It wasn't easy but they got there.

The mayor was relieved and amazed when he arrived at City Hall. He thanked the figure and said: "How could you find the way without any source of light? I couldn't see a thing." The figure sighed and answered, "You see, I am blind, I don't need a light. I am used to finding my way in the dark."

Bishop Taban paused. Then he looked at me and said, "Your people ask how we go on without what you call hope, or light in darkness, or light at the end of the tunnel. What can I tell you and your people, except that God is our blind guide?"

It seems true that true seers are indeed blind.